The Homekeeper's Diary 2021

FRANCIS BRENNAN

Gill Books

Gill Books
Hume Avenue
Park West
Dublin 12
www.gillbooks.ie

Gill Books is an imprint of
M.H. Gill and Co.

978 07171 88741

Edited by Alison Walsh
Designed by iota (www.iota-books.ie)
Portrait photography by Barry Murphy
Styling by Ann Marie O'Leary
Printed by L.E.G.O. SpA, Italy
This book is typeset in Hoefler, DIN
    and Brandon Grotesque

For permission to reproduce photographs,
the author and publisher gratefully
acknowledge the following: © iStock: 28,
35, 60, 64, 74, 80, 86, 98, 112, 118, 140,
144, 150, 164; © Shutterstock: 22.

The author and publisher have made
every effort to trace all copyright
holders, but if any have been
inadvertently overlooked we would
be pleased to make the necessary
arrangement at the first opportunity.

This book is printed on Burgo's Selena
100% PEFC certified and comes from the
wood pulp of managed forests. For every
tree felled, at least one tree is planted,
thereby renewing natural resources.

A CIP catalogue record for this book
is available from the British Library.
5 4 3 2

Name:

Address:

Eircode:

Phone number:

Email address:

Emergency contacts: 1.

2.

About the Author

Francis Brennan is a national treasure and the bestselling author of *It's the Little Things*, *Counting My Blessings*, *Francis Brennan's Book of Household Management* and *A Gentleman Abroad*. He fronts one of Ireland's most popular TV shows, *At Your Service*, and his wit and charm have endeared him to fans across the country. Together with his brother John, he is co-owner of the five-star Park Hotel Kenmare.

CONTENTS

A NOTE FROM FRANCIS

Some of you might know that I spent a lot of time in hospital as a child. I was born with a wonky foot and needed a number of operations to straighten it. During the Christmas of 1966, I was in Cappagh Hospital in Finglas and somebody – I don't remember who – gave me a little diary as a present. Like lots of us, I made a New Year's resolution that I'd write in it, and I did. But then I didn't stop. I have kept on filling diaries to this day.

Every evening, no matter what, I write a couple of lines in my diary. Sometimes, I'll be just about to nod off and remember that I have to do it, so you can imagine how irritating that is! I'll have to switch the bedside light on again and put pen to paper before I can go to sleep. I don't do it for cathartic reasons, but simply as an *aide-memoire*, a process of marking the days and also as a daily discipline – much like a monk might say his prayers or a teacher might mark copybooks. It's a habit, but one that has given me a lot of pleasure over the years.

In December 2018 I was on the road a lot, in London and New York, and I knew that I needed to buy a new diary. Now, I'm very fussy about the format. I like it pocket-sized, week-to-view, with enough room for a couple of lines each day. Nowadays, these are surprisingly difficult to find. I wandered the streets of New York, looking into every stationery shop and department store – and do you think I could find a diary? In London I even looked in that gorgeous posh stationery shop, Smythson. The diaries were a thing of beauty, crafted by hand with lots of lovely extras – but the *price*! I don't think they were in the market for a little pocket diary! On 18 December, I drove to Sligo to visit Mum, and on the outskirts of the town I dropped in to a little petrol station and, lo and behold, there was a stack of little pocket diaries in a rack on the counter. I had travelled the world in search of my diary and here it was in a filling station in Sligo town.

The diary that I've compiled for you is slightly bigger than my own, but I hope that you enjoy the facts, observations and quotes and have a go at the recipes; there is also room for your own reflections, notes or to-do lists. I also wanted to inject some fun into this diary, which is so important after the challenging year we've all had. Whatever you use it for, in our world of technology, the old-fashioned habit of jotting in a diary is an excellent mindfulness exercise. I hope you enjoy it as much as I do.

ESSENTIAL INFORMATION

Health

Doctor	
Dentist	
Health insurance policy number	
PPS number	
Children's PPS numbers	

Name	Number
Name	Number
Name	Number
Name	Number

Local hospital	
Blood group	
Dentist	
Physiotherapist	
EHIC number	expires
Vet	
Pet insurance policy number	

Money

Bank	
Credit union	
Post office	
Credit card helpline	
Overseas credit card helpline	

Around the house

Hairdresser	
Plumber	
Electrician	
Gas company	
Oil supplier	
Nearest garda station	
Home insurance provider	
Home insurance policy number	

Children

Childminder	
School office	
School office	
Children's phone numbers	
Name	Number
Name	Number
Name	Number
Name	Number

Cars

Car registration number		
Breakdown assistance		
Car insurance provider		
Car insurance policy number		
Mechanic		
Nearest NCT testing centre		Test due
Car tax renewal		
Local taxi service		

Work

Office	
Direct line	

Useful websites and numbers

National Car Testing Service	www.ncts.ie	
Department of Foreign Affairs	www.dfa.ie/passportonline/	
Citizens Information	www.citizensinformation.ie	076 107 4000
Irish Rail	www.irishrail.ie	1850 366 222
Bus Eireann	www.buseireann.ie	1850 836 611
Translink NI Railways/Translink Ulsterbus	www.translink.co.uk	028 (048) 9066 6630
Dublin Bus	www.dublinbus.ie	01 873 4222

YEAR AT A GLANCE

JANUARY						
S	M	T	W	T	F	S
					1	2
3	4	5	6	7	8	9
10	11	12	13	14	15	16
17	18	19	20	21	22	23
24	25	26	27	28	29	30
31						

FEBRUARY						
S	M	T	W	T	F	S
	1	2	3	4	5	6
7	8	9	10	11	12	13
14	15	16	17	18	19	20
21	22	23	24	25	26	27
28						

MARCH						
S	M	T	W	T	F	S
	1	2	3	4	5	6
7	8	9	10	11	12	13
14	15	16	17	18	19	20
21	22	23	24	25	26	27
28	29	30	31			

APRIL						
S	M	T	W	T	F	S
				1	2	3
4	5	6	7	8	9	10
11	12	13	14	15	16	17
18	19	20	21	22	23	24
25	26	27	28	29	30	

MAY						
S	M	T	W	T	F	S
						1
2	3	4	5	6	7	8
9	10	11	12	13	14	15
16	17	18	19	20	21	22
23	24	25	26	27	28	29
30	31					

JUNE						
S	M	T	W	T	F	S
		1	2	3	4	5
6	7	8	9	10	11	12
13	14	15	16	17	18	19
20	21	22	23	24	25	26
27	28	29	30			

JULY						
S	M	T	W	T	F	S
				1	2	3
4	5	6	7	8	9	10
11	12	13	14	15	16	17
18	19	20	21	22	23	24
25	26	27	28	29	30	31

AUGUST						
S	M	T	W	T	F	S
1	2	3	4	5	6	7
8	9	10	11	12	13	14
15	16	17	18	19	20	21
22	23	24	25	26	27	28
29	30	31				

SEPTEMBER						
S	M	T	W	T	F	S
			1	2	3	4
5	6	7	8	9	10	11
12	13	14	15	16	17	18
19	20	21	22	23	24	25
26	27	28	29	30		

OCTOBER						
S	M	T	W	T	F	S
					1	2
3	4	5	6	7	8	9
10	11	12	13	14	15	16
17	18	19	20	21	22	23
24	25	26	27	28	29	30
31						

NOVEMBER						
S	M	T	W	T	F	S
	1	2	3	4	5	6
7	8	9	10	11	12	13
14	15	16	17	18	19	20
21	22	23	24	25	26	27
28	29	30				

DECEMBER						
S	M	T	W	T	F	S
			1	2	3	4
5	6	7	8	9	10	11
12	13	14	15	16	17	18
19	20	21	22	23	24	25
26	27	28	29	30	31	

Bank and public holidays in Ireland 2021

Friday 1 January – New Year's Day
Wednesday 17 March – St Patrick's Day
Monday 5 April – Easter Monday
Monday 3 May – May Day bank holiday
Monday 7 June – June bank holiday
Monday 2 August – August bank holiday
Monday 25 October – October bank holiday
Saturday 25 December – Christmas Day
Sunday 26 December – St Stephen's Day

2022

JANUARY
S	M	T	W	T	F	S
						1
2	3	4	5	6	7	8
9	10	11	12	13	14	15
16	17	18	19	20	21	22
23	24	25	26	27	28	29
30	31					

FEBRUARY
S	M	T	W	T	F	S
		1	2	3	4	5
6	7	8	9	10	11	12
13	14	15	16	17	18	19
20	21	22	23	24	25	26
27	28					

MARCH
S	M	T	W	T	F	S
		1	2	3	4	5
6	7	8	9	10	11	12
13	14	15	16	17	18	19
20	21	22	23	24	25	26
27	28	29	30	31		

APRIL
S	M	T	W	T	F	S
					1	2
3	4	5	6	7	8	9
10	11	12	13	14	15	16
17	18	19	20	21	22	23
24	25	26	27	28	29	30

MAY
S	M	T	W	T	F	S
1	2	3	4	5	6	7
8	9	10	11	12	13	14
15	16	17	18	19	20	21
22	23	24	25	26	27	28
29	30	31				

JUNE
S	M	T	W	T	F	S
			1	2	3	4
5	6	7	8	9	10	11
12	13	14	15	16	17	18
19	20	21	22	23	24	25
26	27	28	29	30		

JULY
S	M	T	W	T	F	S
					1	2
3	4	5	6	7	8	9
10	11	12	13	14	15	16
17	18	19	20	21	22	23
24	25	26	27	28	29	30
31						

AUGUST
S	M	T	W	T	F	S
	1	2	3	4	5	6
7	8	9	10	11	12	13
14	15	16	17	18	19	20
21	22	23	24	25	26	27
28	29	30	31			

SEPTEMBER
S	M	T	W	T	F	S
				1	2	3
4	5	6	7	8	9	10
11	12	13	14	15	16	17
18	19	20	21	22	23	24
25	26	27	28	29	30	

OCTOBER
S	M	T	W	T	F	S
						1
2	3	4	5	6	7	8
9	10	11	12	13	14	15
16	17	18	19	20	21	22
23	24	25	26	27	28	29
30	31					

NOVEMBER
S	M	T	W	T	F	S
		1	2	3	4	5
6	7	8	9	10	11	12
13	14	15	16	17	18	19
20	21	22	23	24	25	26
27	28	29	30			

DECEMBER
S	M	T	W	T	F	S
				1	2	3
4	5	6	7	8	9	10
11	12	13	14	15	16	17
18	19	20	21	22	23	24
25	26	27	28	29	30	31

2023

JANUARY
S	M	T	W	T	F	S
1	2	3	4	5	6	7
8	9	10	11	12	13	14
15	16	17	18	19	20	21
22	23	24	25	26	27	28
29	30	31				

FEBRUARY
S	M	T	W	T	F	S
			1	2	3	4
5	6	7	8	9	10	11
12	13	14	15	16	17	18
19	20	21	22	23	24	25
26	27	28				

MARCH
S	M	T	W	T	F	S
			1	2	3	4
5	6	7	8	9	10	11
12	13	14	15	16	17	18
19	20	21	22	23	24	25
26	27	28	29	30	31	

APRIL
S	M	T	W	T	F	S
						1
2	3	4	5	6	7	8
9	10	11	12	13	14	15
16	17	18	19	20	21	22
23	24	25	26	27	28	29
30						

MAY
S	M	T	W	T	F	S
	1	2	3	4	5	6
7	8	9	10	11	12	13
14	15	16	17	18	19	20
21	22	23	24	25	26	27
28	29	30	31			

JUNE
S	M	T	W	T	F	S
				1	2	3
4	5	6	7	8	9	10
11	12	13	14	15	16	17
18	19	20	21	22	23	24
25	26	27	28	29	30	

JULY
S	M	T	W	T	F	S
						1
2	3	4	5	6	7	8
9	10	11	12	13	14	15
16	17	18	19	20	21	22
23	24	25	26	27	28	29
30	31					

AUGUST
S	M	T	W	T	F	S
		1	2	3	4	5
6	7	8	9	10	11	12
13	14	15	16	17	18	19
20	21	22	23	24	25	26
27	28	29	30	31		

SEPTEMBER
S	M	T	W	T	F	S
					1	2
3	4	5	6	7	8	9
10	11	12	13	14	15	16
17	18	19	20	21	22	23
24	25	26	27	28	29	30

OCTOBER
S	M	T	W	T	F	S
1	2	3	4	5	6	7
8	9	10	11	12	13	14
15	16	17	18	19	20	21
22	23	24	25	26	27	28
29	30	31				

NOVEMBER
S	M	T	W	T	F	S
			1	2	3	4
5	6	7	8	9	10	11
12	13	14	15	16	17	18
19	20	21	22	23	24	25
26	27	28	29	30		

DECEMBER
S	M	T	W	T	F	S
					1	2
3	4	5	6	7	8	9
10	11	12	13	14	15	16
17	18	19	20	21	22	23
24	25	26	27	28	29	30
31						

Phases of the Moon

Full Moon	New Moon	Last Quarter	First Quarter
28 January	13 January	6 January	20 January
27 February	11 February	4 February	19 February
28 March	13 March	6 March	21 March
27 April	12 April	4 April	20 April
26 May	11 May	3 May	19 May
24 June	10 June	2 June	18 June
24 July	10 July	1 July 31 July	17 July
22 August	8 August	30 August	15 August
21 September	7 September	29 September	13 September
20 October	6 October	28 October	13 October
19 November	4 November	27 November	11 November
19 December	4 December	27 December	11 December

Lunar events Ireland 2021

Super full Moon – 27 April; 27 May
Super new Moon – 4 November; 4 December
Blue Moon – 22 August
Partial lunar eclipse – 26 May (not visible in Ireland); 19 November
Solar eclipse – 10 June; 4 December (not visible in Ireland)

Names for the Moon throughout the year

January – Wolf Moon
February – Snow Moon
March – Worm Moon
April – Pink Moon
May – Flower Moon
June – Strawberry Moon
July – Buck Moon
August – Sturgeon Moon
September – Harvest Moon
October – Hunter's Moon
November – Beaver Moon
December – Cold Moon

Sunrise and sunset times

Dublin	Sunrise	Sunset
1 January 2021	08.40	16.16
1 February 2021	08.10	17.07
1 March 2021	07.13	18.02
1 April 2021	06.59	19.59
1 May 2021	05.51	20.53
1 June 2021	05.04	21.41
1 July 2021	05.03	21.54
1 August 2021	05.42	21.18
1 September 2021	06.35	20.12
1 October 2021	07.27	19.00
1 November 2021	07.24	16.51
1 December 2021	08.18	16.09

Cork	Sunrise	Sunset
1 January 2021	08.42	16.33
1 February 2021	08.13	17.21
1 March 2021	07.20	18.13
1 April 2021	07.09	20.06
1 May 2021	06.05	20.57
1 June 2021	05.21	21.42
1 July 2021	05.20	21.55
1 August 2021	05.57	21.21
1 September 2021	06.47	20.19
1 October 2021	07.36	19.10
1 November 2021	07.29	17.04
1 December 2021	08.20	16.25

Tides 2021

		1 Jan	1 Feb	1 Mar	1 Apr	1 May	1 Jun	1 Jul	1 Aug	1 Sep	1 Oct	1 Nov	1 Dec
Dublin	h/t	03.20 / 15.26	04.03 / 16.14	00.55 / 13.08	02.55 / 15.16	03.18 / 15.51	04.46 / 17.37	05.11 / 17.57	06.05 / 18.49	07.29 / 20.05	08.17 / 20.32	08.41 / 20.47	08.53 / 21.06
	l/t	08.52 / 21.33	9.40 / 22.21	06.17 / 18.46	08.25 / 20.53	09.03 / 21.27	10.54 / 23.12	11.18 / 23.30	12.14	00.55 / 13.33	01.37 / 14.04	01.57 / 14.12	02.06 / 14.24
Cork	h/t	06.38 / 18.56	07.46 / 20.05	06.26 / 19.05	08.48 / 21.10	09.16 / 21.43	10.51 / 23.25	04.53 / 17.16	12.07	00.46 / 13.23	01.22 / 14.06	02.03 / 14.32	02.15 / 15.45
	l/t	00.43 / 13.05	01.52 / 14.16	00.55 / 13.18	02.57 / 15.18	03.23 / 15.44	04.52 / 17.16	11.19 / 23.45	06.05 / 18.30	07.10 / 19.51	07.47 / 20.35	08.27 / 20.59	08.43 / 23.14
Belfast	h/t	00.09 / 12.23	01.19 / 13.31	00.15 / 12.28	02.18 / 14.40	02.45 / 15.18	04.15 / 17.05	04.41 / 17.27	05.27 / 18.20	06.53 / 19.26	07.33 / 19.49	08.01 / 20.05	08.13 / 20.24
	l/t	06.12 / 18.24	07.19 / 19.55	06.18 / 18.50	08.28 / 20.56	09.05 / 21.27	10.48 / 23.03	11.12 / 23.21	12.05	00.37 / 13.10	01.12 / 13.37	01.42 / 13.58	01.55 / 14.15
Galway	h/t	06.16 / 18.42	07.21 / 19.48	06.21 / 18.45	08.23 / 20.47	08.59 / 21.21	10.52 / 23.10	11.15 / 23.28	12.08	00.57 / 13.39	01.59 / 14.18	02.15 / 14.25	02.17 / 14.35
	l/t	12.22	00.59 / 13.26	00.00 / 12.23	02.01 / 14.24	02.34 / 14.57	04.23 / 16.48	04.49 / 17.10	05.41 / 18.13	07.09 / 20.03	08.00 / 20.41	08.09 / 20.31	08.16 / 20.39

HOUSEHOLD BUDGETING

There are many online budgeting tools and my favourite is the MABS (Money Advice and Budgeting Service) tool for calculating a family budget. You'll find it on www.mabs.ie. Before you start, here are a few money-saving tips:

- Shop around for the best offers on home, pet and car insurance. Many suppliers offer discounts if you take out more than one policy. The same applies if you have a no-claims bonus, or don't have any points on your licence.
- Debt has become a part of many people's lives, but if your debts are weighing you down, get help. MABS will give you information on mortgage arrears, credit card debts, etc. and will even contact creditors on your behalf.
- Be realistic about your expenses. If you enjoy a weekly take-away, write it down. The same goes for your daily coffee: it's the only way you'll get a realistic picture.
- Switching power suppliers is easy and lots of them have one-year special offers, so don't pay more than you need for your gas or electricity. The same goes for broadband and TV – there are lots of offers out there, so dig around for the best one.
- Shop carefully. Go alone, if you can, to avoid being pestered to buy more than you need; and don't shop on an empty stomach – then you're less likely to reach for the chocolate biscuits.
- I'm a terrible man for a bargain and I've often ended up buying more than I need because I couldn't resist the special offer, whether I needed it or not. However, snap up any reduced expensive items you might see – like detergents or dishwasher tablets.
- Don't forget to factor in the odd treat – there's no point saving like mad if you're miserable. Life is to be enjoyed.

Here is an example of what a budget planner might include.
You can do one monthly or weekly.

STEP ONE
INCOME

Source	Amount
Total	

STEP TWO
SAVINGS

Saving for	Starting Balance	Amount Added	Ending Balance
Total			

STEP THREE
FIXED EXPENSES

Description	Amount
Total	

STEP FOUR
SUMMARY

Total Income	
Less Total Fixed Expenses	
Less Total Amount to Savings	
Remaining for Variable Expenses	

STEP FIVE
VARIABLE EXPENSES

Description	Amount	Remaining

50-30-20 METHOD

Another easy way to look at your monthly budget is to apply the 50-30-20 rule. This has the advantage of being nice and simple to organise and remember.

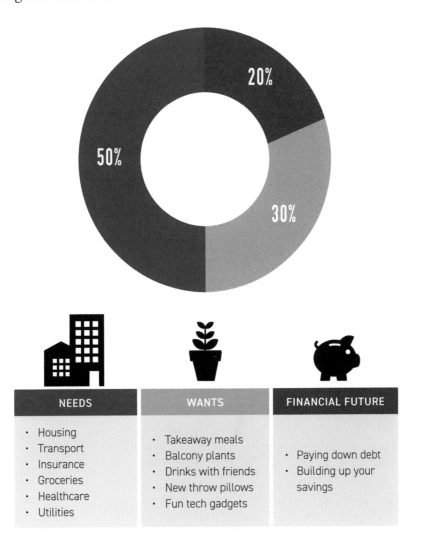

NEEDS	WANTS	FINANCIAL FUTURE
· Housing	· Takeaway meals	· Paying down debt
· Transport	· Balcony plants	· Building up your savings
· Insurance	· Drinks with friends	
· Groceries	· New throw pillows	
· Healthcare	· Fun tech gadgets	
· Utilities		

CONVERSION TABLES

I used to go half mad trying to work out what US cups were in grams and so on, so this handy primer will come in useful for me as well as you! Also, www.onlineconversion.com allows you to convert any measurement.

HEAT

$°C \times 1.8 + 32 = °F$
$°F - 32 / 1.8 = °C$

Gas	°F	°C
¼	250	120
1	275	140
2	300	150
3	325	170
4	350	180
5	375	190
6	400	200
7	425	220
8	450	230
9	475	240

VOLUME

One cup	Imperial	Metric
Caster sugar	8oz	225g
Brown sugar	6oz	170g
Butter	8oz	115g
Flour	5oz	140g
Raisins	7oz	200g
Syrup	12oz	340g

1 TEASPOON = 5ML
1 DESSERTSPOON = 10ML
1 TABLESPOON = 15ML

WEIGHT
1KG = 35OZ/2.2LB

LIQUIDS

Imperial	Metric
½oz	15g
¾oz	20g
1oz	30g
2oz	60g
3oz	85g
4oz (¼lb)	115g
5oz	140g
6oz	170g
7oz	200g
8oz (½lb)	230g
9oz	255g
10oz	285g
11oz	310g
12oz (¾lb)	340g
13oz	370g
14oz	400g
15oz	425g
16oz (1lb)	450g
24oz	680g
32oz (2lb)	0.9kg
48oz (3lb)	1.4kg
64oz (4lb)	1.8kg

Pint	Metric	Cup	fl. oz
	100ml		3½
	125ml	½	4½
¼	150ml		5
	200ml		7
	250ml	1	9
½	275ml		10
	300ml		11
	400ml		14
	500ml	2	18
1	570ml		20
	750ml	3	26
1¾	1.0l	4	35

WASHING SYMBOLS

Last year, with no launderettes or dry cleaners open, I became an expert in the art of handwashing and fabric care. Here's a handy primer on the most common symbols.

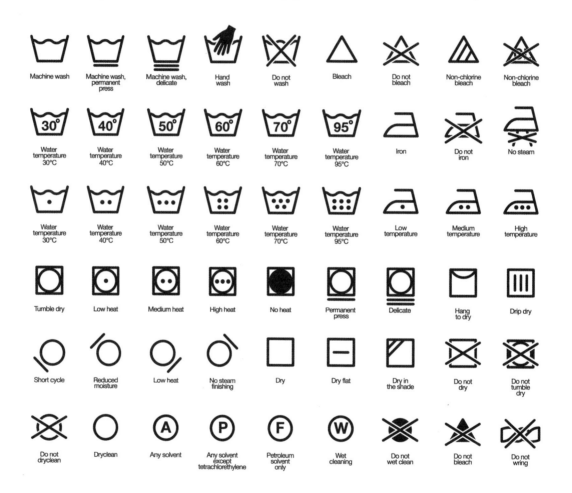

CARING FOR FABRICS

The other thing I learned last year – the hard way – was how to care for delicate fabrics. I had a couple of accidents with shrinking items of clothing, so now I'm careful to (a) check the label and (b) look up a 'how to' so my precious delicates don't end up a shrivelled mess. Here's a handy table of the most common fabrics and how to care for them.

WOOL	SILK	COTTON
Have you ever put a woollen jumper in the wash and taken it out to discover it's like a little ball of felt? I have. Wool should be washed in lukewarm water with a gentle detergent. Don't knead it vigorously or wring it out – a gentle squeeze is best, before shaping your damp woollen item and drying it flat. A friend of mine pops her jumpers in a colander and lets them drip away before doing this, which is very clever.	Again, lukewarm water is best, and a specialist detergent – but before you wash, do a patch test to check that your garment is colour-fast. Dampen a little corner of the item and press it into a white towel – if the colour comes off, you'll need to have it dry-cleaned.	I used to wash my cottons in a hot wash, before I discovered that not all cottons are the same. So my nice 100 per cent cotton shirt needs a cold wash, but my cotton bedsheets, underwear and bath towels need a hot one to get rid of any nasties. I also don't tumble dry cotton clothes, because they shrink, and I turn them inside out before washing to preserve them better.

LINEN	ATHLEISURE
I love linen, because it's a gorgeous fabric and it's not that hard to look after. Lukewarm water is your friend, along with a mild detergent. You can wash it in the machine (although I'd get linen jackets dry-cleaned because of their shape and because the lining might shrink) on a delicates setting. Dry your linens flat and iron while damp. Don't iron them when fully dry or you'll fix the creases.	Nowadays, so many of us wear this not only to the gym but also in everyday life. However, you don't need to wash it on a hot cycle to get rid of bacteria – if you do, the garments won't last. Cold water is your friend, and provided you wash your garments after exercise and reasonably frequently, germs should not be an issue. A pre-soak with half a cup of white vinegar in cold water will really help with odour. Don't use fabric softener on athleisure, because it damages the fibres, and don't dry-clean it. Instead, roll it in a towel to absorb moisture and then dry it flat.

FRANCIS'S HANDY HOW TO ...

Change a plug

1. Unscrew the centre screw on your plug with a Phillips-head screwdriver.
2. Now loosen the two screws at the bottom – the ones that hold the cable in place.
3. Remove the little clamp.
4. Check carefully which wires go into which terminal – *before* you loosen each terminal using a flat-head screwdriver. Green and yellow – earth; brown – live; blue – neutral. Remove the wires.
5. Prepare the new plug by opening it in the same way as you did the old one.
6. Prepare the wires for the new plug. You might need to strip some of the casing off the wires using pliers, but don't cut into the wires themselves. Arrange the wires in the correct positions for each terminal.

7. Snip a tiny bit off the wires so that you see the copper, which you then twist before placing in each terminal. Again, make sure the correct wire is in the correct terminal!

8. Screw the terminals down onto the copper wire, then press the flex into the relevant slot – the flex, not the wires – before tightening the clamp, screwing it over the flex, then snapping both sides of the plug together and tightening the external screw.

Descale a kettle

1. Simply fill your kettle before going to bed with equal parts white vinegar and water.
2. Leave overnight and rinse thoroughly in the morning.
3. Fill the kettle with fresh water and boil it before using.

Clean a washing machine

1. Give the plastic seal a good scrub with a solution of vinegar and water.
2. Pour 500 ml of vinegar into the drum (it won't harm it).
3. Mix equal amounts of baking soda and water (about 50 ml of each) and add this to your detergent drawer.
4. Set your machine to do a hot wash (making sure it's empty!).
5. When it's finished, look inside to check for any gunge, which you can easily wipe away. Don't forget to give the detergent drawer a good wipe as well.

Clean a laptop

Always check your computer manual before you undertake any cleaning.

1. Unplug your device.
2. For the screen, your best bet is a specialist screen cleaner. Don't use Windolene or anything like it – it's not suitable for laptop or PC screens.
3. For the keyboard, I use the brush attachment of my vacuum to very gently remove any dirt. If you have a hand-held cleaner, that would work too.
4. Get a damp sponge and wring it out so that there is absolutely no excess water. Cool boiled water is ideal. Wipe it gently over the keyboard. A cleansing wipe is also useful, provided it does not contain any harsh cleaning abrasives.
5. A cotton swab will work wonders at prising loose dirt from around your keys. Be gentle. Don't lift the keys unless you absolutely have to – they can be tricky to put back.
6. Hoover up any loosened dirt with your brush attachment.
7. You can use a dilute solution of rubbing alcohol dabbed onto a cloth to wipe the case. Again, make sure there are no drips from the cloth. Wipe the case with a dry cloth.
8. Compressed air is brilliant for loosening grime in your USB ports.

Change a lightbulb

1. Make sure the light switch is off. Better still, switch off the electricity at the mains for extra safety.
2. Stand on something secure, like a sturdy chair, if the light fixture is above you.
3. If the bulb is still warm, use a dry cloth to hold it.

4. If the bulb is a bayonet fitting, push it up gently, then twist in an anticlockwise direction to loosen it. If it is a screw fitting, turn it gently anticlockwise until it comes loose.

5. Take the new bulb out of the packaging and insert into the fitting, turning it in a clockwise direction this time. Dispose of the old bulb safely.

Check a fuse

1. Most of us have 'trip-switch' fuses nowadays, instead of the old white fuse box.

2. Turn off your electricity at the mains before you do anything. You'll see it in your fuse box – a larger switch to the side which you pull down into the 'off' position.

3. Now look along the fuses in the fuse box. If you notice that one of the switches is down, it's been 'tripped', or overloaded.

4. Flip the switch back up to reset it – if it doesn't work, check locally to see if there has been a power-cut. If there hasn't been a power-cut, call an electrician to be on the safe side.

SHOPPING LISTS

If saving money is essential, or even if you want to simply waste less, consider making a grocery list. Not a scribble on a Post-it note, but something you can update, add to and reshape according to your needs. You can do this by food category (e.g. 'meat', 'pulses', 'dairy', etc.) or by meal planning and buying accordingly. Either way, it's a good idea to have on hand a list of things you always need or don't need. I currently have three jars of coffee and two pats of butter because I didn't take my own advice! A few tips:

- Plan your meals for the week so you know exactly what to buy.
- Decide what your spending priorities are, whether it's organic meat or fresh fish, and buy the best quality that you can afford.
- Keep your larder stocked with basics so there's always something on standby. 'Margaret's Larder' in April in the diary will help you with this.
- Plan your weekly budget in advance. I'm shopping for one, so it's easy for me. If you have a family, your needs will be greater – but you can still save by buying certain high-cost items, like shampoo and washing detergents, when there's an offer on.
- Familiarise yourself with the aisles of your local supermarket to see what's in stock and how much it costs. Look at the *price per kg* to assess this. A 2kg bag of apples might cost less than a tray of four, depending on brand.
- If budget is a factor, stock up on tinned pulses and staples like rice and pasta. We all need fresh fruit and veg, but it can be easily wasted. I like to use up all my spare veg on a meat-free Monday.
- I'm a divil for getting distracted in the shop by the lovely things on display, but I have to force myself to stick to the list!

- Look for cheaper or 'own brand' versions of items like tinned tomatoes, where quality isn't such an issue – that leaves you more to spend on other things.
- Nominate one or two days in the month for using up everything in the cupboard, before buying more.

Your 'master' meal plan and grocery list might look like this:

SUNDAY	
MONDAY	
TUESDAY	
WEDNESDAY	
THURSDAY	
FRIDAY	
SATURDAY	

PRODUCE	BREAD/BAKERY	DELI	BREAKFAST

BAKING GOODS	CANNED GOODS	CONDIMENTS	SNACKS

REFRIGERATED	MEAT/SEAFOOD	FROZEN	DRINKS

HEALTH/BEAUTY	HOUSEHOLD	MISC	

FOOD SUBSTITUTES

Many of us nowadays choose to eat a vegetarian or even vegan diet. Some of us have food intolerances or simply don't like the taste of, say, eggs. And, if you're like me, you reach for the baking powder in the cupboard and discover you've run out. Here's a list of substitutes for commonly used items:

Egg white	Aquafaba (the water from a can of chickpeas), 2tbsp per egg white. It works!
Whole egg	1tbsp ground flax seeds mixed with 3tbsp water per egg.
Flour	Almond flour; sorghum flour; oat flour; chickpea flour; coconut flour. If you are baking with these, you'll need to experiment as they won't give exactly the same results as wheat flour. I used spelt flour in a loaf recently and it was lovely, but crumblier than one made with wheat flour. You can use ground almonds or polenta very successfully in cakes. To thicken a stew, use a slice or two of potato instead of flour.
Buttermilk	Add 1tbsp lemon juice per 250ml of whole/half-fat milk.
Soured cream	Crème fraîche; double cream with a teaspoon of lemon juice added.
Salt	Soy sauce or a crushed stock cube in soups or stews.
Butter	In baking, use flavourless oils, coconut oil or margarine in a block (not spread); or the equivalent amount of unsweetened stewed apple if you want to go low fat.
Lemon/orange juice	Plain vinegar (in salad dressings).
Vinegar	Brine from jarred pickles.

Sugar	Honey, maple syrup, agave nectar. Try baking with sweet root veg such as beetroot or sweet potato. Beetroot is great with chocolate in a cake.
Rice	Quinoa, buckwheat, bulgur wheat.
Mince in a burger	Jackfruit; pulses such as chickpeas, kidney beans, butter beans.
Potato	Other root veg such as parsnips or carrots; cauliflower.
Baking powder	To replace 1tsp baking powder – ¼tsp baking soda + ½tsp cream of tartar.
Breadcrumbs	Cream-cracker crumbs.
Brown sugar	Granulated sugar + molasses or treacle (1tbsp per 8oz/250g).
Cream cheese	Cottage cheese or ricotta, whipped smooth.
Red wine (in cooking!)	Cider; tomato juice; water.
White wine	Apple juice.
Worcestershire sauce	Soy sauce.
Vanilla essence	Dark rum; maple syrup.
Double cream	In soups and stews, single cream or even full-fat milk is fine; crème fraîche has a similar fat content. In baking, try one part melted butter to three parts milk, whisked. Coconut cream is an excellent vegan substitute. Mascarpone contains even more fat than double cream, so it makes a nice cake topping.
Stock	Dried mushrooms, soaked in boiling water.
Parmesan	Fried breadcrumbs, well seasoned; cheaper alternatives such as Grana Padano.
Chocolate	In baking: three parts cocoa to one part butter, mixed.

COOKING AND STORING FOOD

When my mother was cooking for the five of us and Dad, she had a meal for every day of the week. My brother John used to call Monday's dinner – leftovers from the Sunday roast – 'the lonely dinner'; Tuesday was stew; Wednesday, bacon and cabbage; Thursday was lamb's liver, Friday was fish, of course, and Saturday was a stuffed pork loin. On Sunday, we always ate a roast, but rarely chicken, which was a luxury in those days. We did eat well, as you can see, and there was no processed food. Nowadays, we eat less meat, which is a good thing, I think. So, what if you want to cook from scratch? How can you cook and store safely? www.safefood.eu is home to advice on food safety. Here are some tips:

Cooking meat

- **Whole cuts** like steak don't have to be cooked all the way through, because the bacteria sit on the outside. However, minced meat needs to be cooked all the way through, as does chicken and pork.
- **Cook your steak** on a very high heat to 'sear' it (and kill bacteria) on the outside, so the inside is nice and pink.
- **Cook chicken thoroughly**. Mum's mantra was always 20 minutes per pound weight plus 20 minutes – i.e. 20 minutes per 450g plus 20 minutes. Check that the chicken's cooked by piercing it with a skewer at the thickest point, like the thigh, and check that the juices run clear. If in doubt, slice into it and check that there are no traces of pink.
- **Defrosting chicken** should take 24 hours for a 2.5kg bird – in the fridge. Put any defrosting meat on a large plate to catch any drips that could get onto food below.

- **Hens' eggs** can be eaten raw (if you really must!), say in mayonnaise, or lightly cooked, if you are a healthy adult. Older people, babies and the immuno-compromised should not eat raw eggs. Duck eggs have a higher risk of salmonella, so cook these thoroughly – in 'raw-egg' recipes, like mayonnaise or tiramisu, use hens' eggs.
- **Use separate chopping boards for meat and vegetables**.
- **Wash your hands** thoroughly before and after handling food.

Foods where extra care is needed

Homemade stock Chill quickly and then put it in the fridge. Make sure it's piping hot if reheating.

Shellfish Only buy shellfish from a trusted source; cook it as fresh as you can; discard any with *open shells* before you cook them. When they are cooked, discard any with *unopened* shells. Oysters should be plump and shiny and retreat from your finger when you poke them.

Raw milk and cheese Don't serve to elderly people or youngsters. Pregnant women should avoid them because of the risk of listeria bacteria.

Rice Cook it properly, serve it quickly. If you are reheating it, cool it down quickly, because bacteria can grow at room temperature – I spread it out on a tea tray to cool it, then refrigerate it immediately. When reheating it, make sure it's piping hot. Only reheat rice once.

Chilled foods These need to be handled with more care than frozen foods, because they go off more quickly. Pay attention to the 'use by' dates on these products. Pack/bag them separately from the rest of your shop, so they don't get warm. Store in the fridge – away from fresh foods – and make sure you use them by the 'use by' date. Cook chilled foods until they are piping hot.

Fish Buy fish that is as fresh as can be – nice bright eyes and a shiny skin are good signs of freshness. You don't have to cook it all the way through. According to www.safefood.eu the bacteria is on the outside of the fish, so the inside can be 'pink' if the outside is well cooked.

RECYCLING – THINGS YOU MIGHT NOT KNOW

- Did you know that soft plastics can't be recycled? They need to go in the bin.
- You can recycle tins, papers, cardboard and rigid plastics.
- Rigid plastics, like bottles, yoghurt cartons, as well as tins, need to be cleaned first as contamination is a big problem in recycling. If you have one dirty container in a batch, it can contaminate the whole lot.
- Make sure that you don't squish everything in. www.mywaste.ie suggests that your recycling should be 'clean, dry and loose'.
- For electronic devices, consult WEEE Ireland at www.weeeireland.ie/household. They have a handy map of centres and retailers where your waste electrical devices can be taken.
- You can donate matching pairs of old shoes (I tie mine together at the laces), clothes and certain soft furnishings (not old sheets or pillowcases) to charity shops. Clothes banks will take more damaged items, which will be shredded and recycled.
- Many councils now offer furniture-removal services for some large items. There is a fee, but it beats a fine for littering!
- There used to be a 'little man' in every street in Ireland who repaired hoovers, washing machines, cookers, even televisions. Those days are gone, but, thankfully, the idea of repairing rather than replacing is taking off again. www.repairmystuff.ie provides a list of places that will repair your devices – everything from lawnmowers to laptops.
- Freetrade Ireland – www.freetradeireland.ie – is a forum on which you can place unwanted items that you want to give away. When I looked at it recently, it contained everything from sofas to topsoil!

- According to MyWaste, Ireland is Europe's top producer of plastic. Oh dear. Let's all try to improve on that. I, for one, have become much more aware of using a 'keep cup' for coffee and a reusable bottle for water, as well as remembering to carry a little tote bag with me to the local shops.
- Your local healthfood store will often have 'refill stations' where you can fill up on household products. Also, refill stores have begun to appear, where you can buy food in bulk. Online stores are great for bulk-buying, say, shampoo, but make sure that the formula works for you before you buy five litres of it.
- I didn't realise how fast 'fast fashion' really is. Some of the larger retailers get daily shipments of new clothes and you can get catwalk looks within a matter of weeks. And most of what we buy is later dumped. So what can we do about it? In Dublin the Rediscovery Centre, 'the National Centre for the Circular Economy' (www.rediscoverycentre.ie), gives classes in sewing, repairs and even knitting. Sustainable fashion brands help us to shop without a guilty conscience, but many of them are more expensive. Look for pre-loved clothing: it's not just for the charity shops any more – there are some very good online sources of pre-loved wedding dresses, bags, shoes and even designer handbags.

Tips for buying pre-loved clothing

- Do your homework. Look carefully at all the websites and apps to check what they are selling, the quality and price. Get to know the best retailers. Some of the larger ones have quality controls to make sure your item is in good shape.
- Vintage clothing can often be smaller than we're used to, so a size 12 jacket might be a size 8 in today's world. Don't be afraid to ask if the item can be altered.

- Make your dressmaker your best friend. A friend of mine is very small, so she's used to having things taken up and in. You'd be amazed what they can do.
- Check to see a seller's feedback if you're buying online – they must have positive reviews and offer great customer service.
- Look closely at the item to check for any damage, staining or wear.
- Don't buy a ton of clothing from, say, a charity shop just because it's cheap. If you won't wear it, don't buy it.

Eco-friendly alternatives to common household items

Make-up removal pads	Homemade fabric pads or recycled bamboo rewashable pads
Make-up cleansers	Solid make-up removal bars (you can also get shampoo bars)
Cotton buds	Biodegradable, bamboo or thin paper cotton buds
Paper kitchen towels	Old bits of cloth
Batteries	Rechargeable batteries
Plastic rubbish/ dog-poo bags	Biodegradable rubbish/poo bags
Bleach	Baking soda + vinegar
Furniture polish	Beeswax
Disposable razors	Safety razor
Baking parchment	Reusable baking inserts (from kitchen stores and online); available in different sizes

Cling film	Reusable food wraps/jar covers made with beeswax – you can make your own jar covers, which can be washed and reused. My mother used paper jar covers, secured with an elastic band, on jars of jam
Plastic food boxes	Stainless-steel containers; Mason jars; bamboo lunchboxes
Paper napkins	Fabric napkins
Plastic straws	Stainless steel or bamboo straws
Coffee pods	Compostable coffee pods – but they are expensive. Better still, use ground coffee in a percolator.
Tea bags	Loose tea leaves
Plastic bottles of water	Reusable water bottle made of stainless steel or glass (with a protective sleeve for breakages)

My best recycled and eco-friendly products

DAYS OUT AROUND IRELAND

Need to take the kids out for the day, or travelling further afield? Here are some ideas:

Dublin and Leinster

- *St Michan's Mummies,* Church Street, Dublin 7. Founded in 1095, St Michan's church is full of history. Its famous vaults house the remains of seventeenth-century Dubliners, preserved because of the limestone. Sadly, you can't touch them any more, but you can have a good look. Bram Stoker was inspired by St Michan's when he wrote *Dracula.*
- *St Anne's City Farm and Ecology Centre*, Raheny – a real glimpse of farm life for city kids. They can admire hens, goats, chickens and pigs as well as learn about growing produce. And it's free! www.stannescityfarm.ie
- *Newbridge House and Farm,* Donabate, is another working farm and you can visit the grounds as well as the house. There's also an adventure playground. www.newbridgehouseandfarm.com
- The *Dead Zoo* – also known as the Natural History Museum, Merrion Square, Dublin 2. The creepy exhibits will entertain your children for hours and it's another free activity. The *Museum at Collins Barracks* has excellent interactive displays to amuse and engage and the bog bodies at the National Museum of Ireland are not to be missed. www.museum.ie
- The *National Print Museum* in Beggars Bush has lots of workshops and classes in printing, organises exhibitions and has an excellent café. www.nationalprintmuseum.ie
- *Powerscourt Estate*, Co. Wicklow – lots to do here (activities are separately ticketed), with the waterfall, the gardens, the

distillery and the Cool Planet Experience, a climate action exhibition. www.powerscourt.com

- *Newgrange*, Co. Meath. I can still remember visiting Newgrange years ago and being able to walk straight across the fields to the site. Nowadays, it's a lot more organised, but a day trip is well worth the effort, with a shuttle bus to ferry you between the sites, a guided tour and exhibits. Amazing to think that it was built 3,200 years BC – before the pyramids and Stonehenge! www.worldheritageireland.ie. Don't forget to visit the Hill of Tara on your way home. It's so atmospheric.
- *Lough Boora* is a lovely discovery park in Tullamore, Co. Offaly, full of ponds and wildlife as well as the remains of the former Bord na Móna peatworks. You can walk on the many trails, hire bikes and there's a café and visitors' centre. www.loughboora.com
- *Athlone Castle*, Co. Westmeath, an impressive castle smack bang on the River Shannon, was defended by Colonel Richard Grace from the Williamite forces after the Battle of the Boyne. www.athlonecastle.ie
- *Sean's Bar* in Athlone is the oldest pub in Ireland, having been in existence for a thousand years. www.seansbar.ie
- *Hodson Bay*, Lough Ree, Co. Westmeath – a friend of mine brought her children to Baysports, an open-air water park, for the day and recommended it. You can also hire kayaks. www.baysports.ie

Connacht

- *The Glen*, Culleenamore, Co. Sligo. A little valley stuffed full of flora and fauna on the side of Knocknarea mountain. You can climb the mountain easily and visit Queen Maeve's grave.

- The 'Lake Isle of Innisfree' can be viewed from a boat trip on Lough Gill, in the area where my mother lived for many years. I also love to visit Drumcliff while I'm in Co. Sligo, where Yeats is buried. The churchyard is idyllic, with its view of Ben Bulben. My brother Damien has transformed my mother's family farm into a homestead and does a tour called the 'Yeats Experience' – www.yeatssligoireland.com
- Mullaghmore, Co. Sligo – a mecca for watersports enthusiasts, with Bundoran and Strandhill beaches close by.
- Mayo Greenway, Westport – this track between Westport and Achill Island is spectacular and winds along for 42km of lovely safe cycling. You can also walk from Newport to Bangor Erris on a walking trail.
- The Erris peninsula is a haven for watersports and UISCE provides tuition as gaeilge in kayaking, windsurfing and so on.
- If you like island-hopping. Inishmaan is the quietest of the Aran islands – an alternative to Inis Mór (the site of Dún Aonghasa), which can be busy in summer. Inishmaan is home to Teach Synge, the restored cottage of playwright John Millington Synge. Inishbofin is also a lovely day trip from Cleggan pier, in Connemara. Ferries leave regularly from the pier to the island, which is tiny, but packed with history and activities, including a regatta and an arts festival.

Munster

- Of course I'm biased about my adopted home of Kerry, but it has lots to offer! Skellig Michael has become such a draw over the last few years, but if you want to see beehive huts without the sheer drop, take a detour to Fahan, on the Dingle peninsula, where you can see other examples of these amazing little houses. You can visit Derrynane House, home of Daniel O'Connell, and there's a lovely beach nearby. www.derrynanehouse.ie. If you don't fancy the Cliffs of Moher, I like the cliffs in *Portmagee*, which are spectacular and from which you can see the Skelligs. *Cosán na Naomh*, an 18km walk to the foot of Brandon Mountain, is one of five ancient pilgrim paths that make up the 'Irish Camino'.

- If you'd like to see phosphorescence, where the water literally lights up, try night kayaking on *Lough Hyne,* Co. Cork. This lake is well known for the phenomenon. www.atlanticseakayaking.com. West Cork is also a great place for whale-watching. Whale Watch West Cork (whalewatchwestcork.com) and Cork Whale Watch (corkwhalewatch.com) both offer tours to – hopefully – see these magnificent creatures.

- A quirky afternoon visit can be paid to Father Ted's house in Co. Clare, originally known as *Glanquin Farmhouse*. You can book afternoon tea there and pay homage!

- You can't visit Waterford without learning about its Viking heritage. *King of the Vikings* is a virtual reality experience – www.kingofthevikings.com; there's also an impressive museum of all things medieval, *Waterford Treasures* www.waterfordtreasures.com. There is also great food to be found in this part of the world, and Waterford City was voted Ireland's food destination 2019, with its own tapas trail, Waterford Harvest Festival and Dungarvan's food festival in springtime.

Ulster

- Everyone knows that Donegal has some of the best beaches in the country, like *Portsalon* beach, but it also has wonderful ruggedness. *Slieve League* has some of the highest cliffs in

Europe – three times the size of the Cliffs of Moher! The Inishowen peninsula is home to *Malin Head*, Ireland's most northerly point and very windswept and spectacular. *Glenveagh National Park* is huge and full of lovely walking trails.

- Most people are familiar with the highlights of the North Antrim Coast, such as the *Giant's Causeway* and *Dunluce Castle*, but I was in Belfast not so long ago and had a fantastic time. It's a compact city and nice to wander around after you see the *Titanic Experience* and take the children to the brilliant science experience, *W5* – w5online.co.uk. The *Troubles Tour* is a guided walking tour of the city led by both Republican and Loyalist former political prisoners, if you would like insights into the conflict, and *Black Taxi Tours* will offer a drive to the relevant hotspots. I also love the *Botanic Gardens*, home to the *Ulster Museum* – nmni.com.

- *Derry* is a lovely town, steeped in history, and a walk around the old walls of the town will give you a real sense of the place. There's a craft village in the city and the *Museum of Free Derry* tells the story of the city during the Troubles – www.museumoffreederry.org. Not far away is *Mussenden Temple*, on a spectacular cliff overlooking the sea – it was built as a library and based on a temple in Rome.

- Apparently, David Cameron went for a swim in *Lough Erne*, Co. Fermanagh, when the Lough Erne resort hosted the G8 summit in 2013. If that isn't temptation enough, there are many islands to explore in this watery area, including *Devenish Island*, with its sixth-century monastery and round tower. There's a road bridge to *Boa Island* – not named after the snake, but after Badhbh, goddess of war. You can also get to *White Island* via ferry to admire the carvings on the ruined church.

MY TRAVEL NOTES

2021

The Post-Christmas Holiday

It's three days after Christmas and you're still looking at the remains of the blessed turkey! If you've tried the soup, sandwiches and turkey and ham pie, why not try a turkey stir-fry with a nice spicy kick? I love the Indonesian dish nasi goreng, a lovely fried rice dish into which you can throw any amount of protein (turkey, prawns, tofu). Cook your turkey for 2 minutes in a smoking-hot wok, before adding a sliced chilli, a sliced clove of garlic, your choice of veg, chopped into nice thin slivers, stir for another couple of minutes before adding the cooked rice (be careful to cool it down properly). Finally, a couple of additions – soy sauce, which is easy to find, and kecap manis, a thick, sweet version of soy sauce. If you can't find it, substitute 2tsp dark soy sauce with ½tsp sugar for that sweetness. Add a dollop of tomato purée, give it all a stir to combine and add a fried egg on top for extra deliciousness. I could eat it until it comes out of my ears!

28 Monday

'Is cuid den mhuc a drioball.' ('The pig's tail is part of the pig'/'The apple doesn't fall far from the tree.')

29 Tuesday

30 Wednesday

31 Thursday NEW YEAR'S EVE

January

1 Friday HAPPY NEW YEAR!

Athbhliain faoi mhaise (Irish)
Bonne année (French)
Gleðilegt nýtt ár (Icelandic)
S novym godom (Russian)
Hyvää uutta vuotta (Finnish)

2 Saturday

3 Sunday

New Year's Un-resolutions

I used to be a great man for making New Year's resolutions. This year was going to be the year I took up Spanish, learned to swim twenty lengths of the swimming pool, gave up eating biscuits – that kind of thing. Of course, I took to my new projects with great enthusiasm, but found myself giving up by the third week of January. Then one New Year's, I rang my friend Jean in the States and she told me that I was doing it all wrong! 'You need to be realistic, Francis. Make your resolutions bite-sized and doable, not pie in the sky.' So I did. And another tip? Make some nice resolutions, too – add something to your life instead of 'giving up'. If last year's challenges taught me anything, it's that you never know what the future brings, so enjoy the now – relish your friends and family, because they'll get you through anything. And finally, tell everyone what your plans are. If I'm going on a health kick, I tell the world and his mother. That way, I know that if I reach for a chocolate éclair, one of them will be on to me, quick as a flash.

4 Monday

'Be kind whenever possible. It is always possible.'
Dalai Lama

5 Tuesday

6 Wednesday NOLLAIG NA mBAN

Ladies, it's time to put your feet up and let the men look after you, as tradition dictates. Long ago, people believed that all the water in the wells turned into wine at midnight! Happy days.

7 Thursday

8 Friday

Cleaning the oven is a job many of us dread, but after Christmas there's nothing else for it. There are companies that will do it for you – imagine! – but it's easy to do yourself with a nice thick paste of baking soda and water (four parts baking soda to one part water), left on for a half an hour, then scrubbed off.

9 Saturday

10 Sunday

Now's the time for a little reward if you've kept your resolutions for a whole week!

Your Garden Planner

My favourite thing to do at this miserable time of the year is to plan my garden. It's lovely to look forward to the spring to come. I know that not everyone has a big garden like I do, or the time to keep a close eye on it, so here are a few tips:

- I'm like a child with a packet of sweets when I get my hands on a seed catalogue! It's great to know that there are local seed suppliers in Ireland, but check that what you're buying is suitable for your climate and soil. What grows in Kerry might not thrive in Donegal and so on.
- I give any propagation trays and little pots a good wash, to get them ready for the new crop of seeds.
- Many of us nowadays live in apartments with balconies, which is challenging for the gardener. Plants like ivies, ferns, ornamental grasses and boxwood like shade. Bamboo plants make great windshields, as does broom, a pretty yellow bush that's a relative of gorse and hardy as you like.
- I love the growbags that come ready for planting. With one or two of these, placed up a bit off the ground so that they drain, you can grow some delicious microgreens on your balcony or patio during the summer.
- Don't forget to water your balcony plants! They need plenty of regular watering to thrive.

11 Monday

'Music is moonlight in the gloomy night of life.' *Jean Paul Friedrich Richter*

12 Tuesday

13 Wednesday

14 Thursday

15 Friday

Get yourself a filing system and sort all your correspondence into files. If you're like me, you'll have the best part of the previous year to get through. The bonus is, you'll start 2021 with a clean slate.

16 Saturday

17 Sunday

A Little January Hygge

It's a tough time of year, when the winter seems never-ending. Time for a little uplift.

- Read a book, snuggled up on the sofa under a warm blanket, in front of a roaring fire. Make yourself a hot chocolate, give the kids something to do (a little telly won't do much harm) and take half an hour for yourself. Better still, make it a weekly appointment. The ironing and other jobs can wait.

- If you're feeling lonely, give Mum and Dad a call. My mother died in January last year at the age of 97 and I miss her hugely. We used to talk every night, catching up on the news of the day. She had more visitors than the Pope: people would call in to see her every single day and in the summer, visitors from America would consult her because she knew everything there was to know about her little corner of the world.

- There's nothing I like better than watching the birds on a January morning. I have a gang of sparrows that commandeer my bird feeders and it really cheers me up to see them. BirdWatch Ireland (www.birdwatch.ie) does a survey of garden birds every winter and you can take part. The website will give you all the details you need.

18 Monday

Blue Monday can get the best of us down. Be kind to yourself, today of all days. You're doing as well as can be expected; the problems can wait. Take a moment to reflect on what matters most to you in life.

19 Tuesday

20 Wednesday

21 Thursday

22 Friday

23 Saturday

24 Sunday

Think of a project you've always wanted to do – the dreary days of January are the perfect time to get started. Download a language app if you want to brush up on your French; design your dream bathroom (there are lots of online resources to do so); declutter the attic; write the first chapter of your novel.

25 Monday

'Don't worry about being successful, but work toward being significant and the success will naturally follow.' *Oprah Winfrey*

26 Tuesday

27 Wednesday

28 Thursday

Whip up a warming winter soup by sautéing an onion with some finely diced parsnip (about 750g) for ten minutes. Add two teaspoons of curry powder, cook for a minute, then add a litre of stock and let it bubble for 20 minutes before whizzing in a blender. Easy!

29 Friday

30 Saturday

31 Sunday

You've made it to the end of January. Time to give yourself a big pat on the back.

FRANCIS'S FASCINATING FACTS

Lá Fheile Bhríde

When I was a child, St Brigid's Day marked the beginning of spring. We'd all be sitting in the classroom at St Anne's National School in Milltown, looking out at the windswept streets while Sister Mary taught us how to make St Brigid's crosses. First she'd put a diagram up on the board, a series of pictures that looked like ogham or Morse code, illustrating the steps that would be needed to make the crosses. Next, she would dole out a dozen red-and-white striped plastic straws to each of us, and we'd begin, watching her carefully as she twisted and knotted the straws into the shape of a St Brigid's cross. Mine was always a bit of a mess, but I'd take it home proudly and Mum would put it on the mantelpiece along with my older brother Damien's cross, two wobbly things into which we'd poured all our love and attention.

Sister Mary also used to tell us stories about this saint, which had a touch of the supernatural about them. My favourite was the story of the founding of her church in Kildare, in which she'd tricked the King of Leinster into giving her land by asking him for just enough land that could be covered by the cloak she wore around her shoulders. Needless to say, when he agreed, the cloak magically grew, spreading out to cover the countryside.

1 Monday

St Biddy's Day, based on the pagan festival of Imbolc, has been revived in Killorglin, Co. Kerry. People dress up in straw hats and there's a torchlit parade through the village. There's also a King of the Biddies contest!

2 Tuesday

Candlemas Day recalls the Christian feast of the Presentation of Jesus. In the Roman Empire, people lit candles in their houses, hence the name. It is also Groundhog Day in America.

3 Wednesday

4 Thursday

5 Friday

6 Saturday

7 Sunday

Time is that precious commodity that we never seem to have enough of. Would you like to use your time differently? Keep a time diary for a week and see how long you spend working, travelling, watching TV and on your phone. You might be surprised by the results!

All Things Rhubarb

You might have heard about 'forced' rhubarb and seen it in the shops – it's such a joy to spot its bright pink stems. It's created by shrouding the plants in darkness so that they 'force' themselves up to the light. But what to do with it? Not everyone loves the tartness of forced rhubarb as much as I do, so chop the stalks into 4cm pieces (remove the toxic leaves), put a good coating of brown sugar on them, along with a squeeze of orange juice and a dusting of orange zest, into the oven at 200°C/400°F/gas mark 6 for 15 minutes and you have lovely roast rhubarb to eat with custard or cream. Add a little less sugar and the rhubarb's natural sourness can also work with roast meat – pork, for example, which really works with fruit.

I was at a conference recently where they served cocktails made with rhubarb – never was I so glad to be a non-drinker, but they certainly looked impressive! I'm more of a rhubarb crumble man myself. Mix oats (150g), flour (125g) and butter (125g) rubbed between your fingers, add brown sugar (125g), then a dash of cinnamon, leave in the freezer for a few minutes to come together and sprinkle over rhubarb. Pop into the oven for 20 minutes at 190°C/375°F/gas mark 5 until it's lovely and brown. Delicious!

8 Monday

'Spring is nature's way of saying "Let's party".' *Robin Williams*

9 Tuesday

10 Wednesday

Time to plant some seeds! Indoors, in little trays, in a nice warm spot will do for the minute. You can plant your seedlings outside when it's warmer, but beware of late frosts!

11 Thursday

12 Friday

13 Saturday

14 Sunday ST VALENTINE'S DAY

Did you know that the relics of St Valentine are in Whitefriar Street Carmelite Church in Dublin? They were donated to the order by Pope Gregory XVI sometime in the nineteenth century.

Pest Control

One of my favourite books is the American compendium *Country Wisdom & Know-How* and I often consult it. It's large and unwieldy, and the print is tiny, but it contains literally everything you will ever need to know about domestic and garden life. It's actually a manual for self-sufficiency, and it contains such gems as how to skin a rabbit, build a chicken coop and breed livestock, should you need them, but you can also read about beauty tips, making bread, propagating berries, feeding birds – the list is endless. It's terrific on organic gardening too. I've picked up a lot of tips, including being a bit kinder to garden pests. Now, instead of sprinkling awful slug killer around the place, I make beer traps for them, so they can drown happily. Any old cheap lager will do, poured onto the lid of a jam jar and placed strategically in my flower beds. I don't find crushed eggshells work for me, because they get damp so quickly and lose their slug resistance. Another thing I learned is that slugs hate copper, so if you make a line of one-cent pieces around your border, pushing them just below the soil surface, they will be put off crawling over them. Who knew?

15 Monday

'Spring is the time of year when it is summer in the sun and winter in the shade.' *Charles Dickens, Great Expectations*

16 Tuesday

17 Wednesday

18 Thursday

'When the oak flowers before the ash we're in for a splash. When the ash flowers before the oak, we're in for a soak.' *Old Irish saying*

19 Friday

20 Saturday

21 Sunday

When I was a child, visiting Granny in County Sligo, I marvelled at her skill at weather forecasting. She would look out from the kitchen window at the little oak wood on the hill across the field to see how the wind was blowing. If it revealed the undersides of the leaves, that meant it was going to rain!

22 Monday

'It always seems impossible until it's done.' *Nelson Mandela*

23 Tuesday

24 Wednesday

25 Thursday

26 Friday

27 Saturday

The first full moon in February. I often think of my friend who goes open-water swimming with other women to mark the full moon. Can you imagine how cold it would be?

28 Sunday

Spring

Nothing is so beautiful as Spring –
When weeds, in wheels, shoot long and lovely and lush;
Thrush's eggs look little low heavens, and thrush
Through the echoing timber does so rinse and wring
The ear, it strikes like lightnings to hear him sing;
The glassy peartree leaves and blooms, they brush
The descending blue; that blue is all in a rush
With richness; the racing lambs too have fair their fling.

What is all this juice and all this joy?
A strain of the earth's sweet being in the beginning
In Eden garden. – Have, get, before it cloy,
Before it cloud, Christ, lord, and sour with sinning,
Innocent mind and Mayday in girl and boy,
Most, O maid's child, thy choice and worthy the winning.

Gerard Manley Hopkins

1 Monday

'A flower blossoms for its own joy.'
Oscar Wilde

2 Tuesday

3 Wednesday

Time to start weeding the garden and
getting the soil ready for planting.
Boiling, salted water is great for
eliminating weeds on your patio or
in concrete – and it's natural.

4 Thursday

5 Friday

6 Saturday

7 Sunday

Every year, I like to set myself a reading challenge. I'll read one novel and one book of non-fiction every month. If I read three one month and only one the next, so what? It gives me something to aim for and a nice excuse to go into a bookshop.

Soda Bread

When the weather is still a bit unpredictable, an afternoon spent baking with the kids is ideal. My mother used to make jam tarts with us, using leftover pastry from an apple tart, into which we'd spoon home-made jam. Soda bread is another easy-peasy thing to make, or cookies. Scones are a bit of a challenge, though – they need careful handling, so they're tricky for small children. A white soda bread with raisins will hit the spot, or a simple muffin. Here's a recipe for my favourite soda bread, which I spread with butter and jam – a lovely treat.

Ingredients

450g flour (plain is fine, but use 2tsp baking powder – or just 1tsp if you're using self-raising)
1tsp bicarbonate of soda
1 or 2tsp baking powder (see above)
50g caster sugar
pinch of salt
50g butter
100g raisins
275ml buttermilk
1 egg

Method

1. Preheat the oven to 170°C/325°F/gas mark 3.
2. Sieve the flour, bicarb and baking powder into a large mixing bowl. Add the sugar and salt and mix well. Add the butter and rub in, using your fingertips, until the mixture looks like breadcrumbs. Add the raisins.
3. In another bowl, whisk the buttermilk with the egg, then pour into the dry ingredients. Mix just until combined – don't overdo it.
4. Tip the mix out onto a well-floured surface and give it a little knead – again, a light touch is needed.
5. Shape it into a round, cut a deep cross into it and place onto a greased baking tray for 40–45 minutes.

8 Monday

'Bloom where you are planted.'
St Francis de Sales

9 Tuesday

10 Wednesday

11 Thursday

Have you tried using dishwasher tablets for cleaning the oven? All you need to do is rub one around a dampened oven and it'll lift the grime away.

12 Friday

13 Saturday

14 Sunday

FRANCIS'S FASCINATING FACTS

St Patrick's Day

This festival has become a global event over the last few years. When I was a child, it consisted of Mass, which we'd attend with a great lump of shamrock in our lapels, followed by the bus into town to watch the parade. And that was it! There was no five-day celebration, nothing was lit up in green and there were certainly no pints of green Guinness! I decided to take a closer look into the day and uncovered a few facts:

- The reason we celebrate it on 17 March is because St Patrick is thought to have died on that date, in AD 461.
- He didn't actually banish snakes from Ireland, because they never actually got here! But it's a good story.
- The first St Patrick's Day parade took place in Boston in 1737.
- In my home county of Kerry, Dingle is the first place to hold a parade – at six o'clock in the morning! In Sneem, the parade often has a political spin, with a dash of satire.
- The colour associated with St Patrick nowadays is green, of course, but originally it was blue. In fact, blue was the colour of the Irish state – and the national football team wore blue jerseys until 1931.

15 Monday

For the planet's sake, I've opted for Meat-Free Mondays. Give it a try. A simple tomato pasta is quick, healthy and tasty, and I can now whip up a veggie green curry with green peppers, peas and spinach and a can of low-fat coconut milk in fifteen minutes. I'm learning!

16 Tuesday

17 Wednesday ST PATRICK'S DAY

18 Thursday

19 Friday

Self-care is so important. Eat well, get some exercise and a good night's sleep. You deserve it.

20 Saturday

21 Sunday

22 Monday

'Knowing yourself is the beginning of all wisdom.' *Aristotle*

23 Tuesday

24 Wednesday

It's window-cleaning time at my home near Sneem. I get the bucket out, fill it with hot water, into which I squeeze a drop or two of washing-up liquid, and off I go. I rinse with clean water. Inside, vinegar will do brilliantly, applied with newspaper and polished to a shine.

25 Thursday

26 Friday

27 Saturday

28 Sunday

FRANCIS'S FASCINATING FACTS

Whipping the Herring

After weeks of fasting and making do on a diet of potatoes and dried fish, you can imagine how much we looked forward to Easter Sunday, when we could gorge on eggs and boiled bacon. First, though, it was time to punish the poor herring for keeping us alive during Lent. A dead fish was hung from a pole and paraded through the streets, to be dumped unceremoniously in the river. The mouldy fish would be replaced by a spring lamb, which had been butchered and dressed in ribbons. I found this funny piece on the ceremony in Drogheda in the local newspaper:

> *The ritual usually got underway early on Easter Sunday morning in a lane way off West Street, now known as Meat Market Lane. Here, the butcher boys assembled and tied dozens of herring to a long light rope which one of the boys would fling over his shoulder. The boy would constantly flog the fish until not a trace was left on the rope. The butcher's boy, who for years shouldered the rope of a herring, was known locally as 'Jimmy the Melt'. He was a man of great physique and had served in the Peninsular war.*

29 Monday

'One touch of nature makes the whole
world kin.' *William Shakespeare*, Troilus
and Cressida

30 Tuesday

31 Wednesday

April

1 Thursday HOLY THURSDAY

2 Friday GOOD FRIDAY

3 Saturday EASTER SATURDAY

4 Sunday EASTER SUNDAY

Try serving leg of lamb with a fresh herb
pesto. Mix 2–3 handfuls of mint and basil (or
rosemary) with a handful of pine nuts and a
clove of garlic. Add salt, enough olive oil to
loosen, and whizz in a blender. Rub it into
the scored skin of the lamb before cooking.

Beetroot Bonanza

April in the garden is a wonderful time, when you'll begin to see the fruits of your January planting. You can also head outdoors, to your balcony, patio or garden, to sow beetroot. Not hard to grow at all in Irish soil and easy-peasy in pots, so perfect for the micro-gardener. And it's very 'now'. You'll find the round varieties suit pots – choose pots that are at least 20x20cm so there's plenty of room for the roots to grow. Fill each pot with compost, almost, but not quite, to the top. Pop your seeds into the soil, leaving a bit of room for each to grow, then cover with 2cm of compost. When the seedlings grow, thin them out, leaving a 10cm gap between them. Don't pull the weaker plants out, as you might disturb the healthy ones: simply pinch the top off them. Keep your weeds down and water regularly in dry weather. There's no need to soak the plants, though – beetroot don't like being soggy! Test the compost with your finger: if it's dry to the touch, give it a little water.

5 Monday EASTER MONDAY BANK HOLIDAY

'Nature does not hurry, yet everything is accomplished.' *Lao Tzu*

6 Tuesday

7 Wednesday

8 Thursday

9 Friday

10 Saturday

11 Sunday

*Just two things. I used
to have endless to-do lists
until I found this handy
tip: think of two things
you need to do today, this
week and this month.
That focuses the mind ...*

Margaret's Larder

My colleague and friend Margaret keeps a fully stocked larder so that if someone lands at her door she can whip up an easy meal or a pudding in no time. It might sound old-fashioned, but if you put effort into your larder, you'll never have to worry about dinner. Everything you need will be there. Essentials in a well-stocked larder include:

- Good jarred sauces for emergency dinners – soy, pesto and teriyaki.
- Tins of chickpeas, kidney beans and other pulses.
- Eggs – I like to store them in the larder as they work better for baking at room temperature.
- Couscous, polenta, pasta, rice – the basis for any quick and easy meal.
- Tinned tomatoes, baked beans for a quick supper on toast, tuna (ditto), sardines, anchovies (not essential, but I like them on pizza and chopped through pasta).
- Spices – paprika, chilli powder, coriander, cumin, cinnamon. Make sure they don't go stale.
- Vanilla/almond essence.
- Sugar and flour – pop a bay leaf in your bag of flour because weevils hate it.
- Oil and vinegar – extra-virgin olive oil for salads, plain for cooking; sunflower oil, white wine vinegar, cider vinegar for dressings.
- Preserves – but store opened jars in the fridge, to guard against mould.

12 Monday

13 Tuesday

14 Wednesday

15 Thursday

16 Friday

17 Saturday

18 Sunday

Get into the garden and clean the deck and barbecue – the prospect of using them both on a sunny day will make it worthwhile! I make a dilute solution of Jeyes Fluid and scrub the deck like mad.

Spring-Cleaning Time!

The weather is now bright enough to show every speck of dust and every streaky window, so a spring clean is just the ticket to freshen up the place before the warmer weather (when you'll want to be outside, not cleaning the bathroom grout with a toothbrush ...). In Victorian times a spring clean was essential, because people were shut up indoors for the whole winter with coal fires burning, so you can imagine the dust and the grime that would have accumulated. Because of this, the Victorians put every stick of furniture and all carpets and bedding outside to 'air' on a nice warm day and set to scrubbing everything. They even whitewashed the walls. Nowadays, you don't need to go quite so far, but the essentials are worth doing and worth doing well, so that your home is sparkling clean and you feel much better as a result. But ...

- Don't try to tackle the whole thing at once. Take one room, or one item, at a time and focus on that.
- Get together all the materials you'll need for the job – from bin liners to cleaning products. Which reminds me, I recently heard a podcast where a young man was remembering his childhood, in particular his mother recycling his father's old underpants to use as dusters! Thank God for microfibre cloths!
- Make a checklist and tick it off as you go – the satisfaction will be all the greater.

19 Monday

20 Tuesday

21 Wednesday

22 Thursday

23 Friday

24 Saturday

25 Sunday

26 Monday

'Surely it is more generous to forgive and remember than to forgive and forget.' *Maria Edgeworth*

27 Tuesday

28 Wednesday

29 Thursday

30 Friday

1 Saturday MAY DAY OR BEALTAINE

May

When I was a child, we'd take off to the banks of the old Harcourt railway line to collect the cowslips that grew on the steep slopes. We'd take them home, tie a string between two chairs to keep it taut, then thread the flowers on – when it was packed, we'd pull it together to form a football shape, which we'd bring into school for the May altar.

2 Sunday

FRANCIS'S FASCINATING FACTS

Bealtaine

I can still remember the May processions in school, walking around the schoolyard with a statue of Holy Mary, saying decades of the Rosary. There was fierce competition to be the statue-bearers, needless to say.

Of course, like so many Christian festivals, May Day has its roots in pagan times. Bealtaine heralded the beginning of summer and would traditionally have been marked by setting a bonfire. People would also create stone circles that would align with the sunrise and sunset. I came across some 'interesting' Bealtaine traditions, such as the 'May baby', in my research. According to archaeology. ie, 'In this curious custom a figure of a female (the May baby) was placed on a pole and then covered in flowers, ribbons and straw. A man and a woman, also dressed up in costume, would then dance around the figure and make vulgar displays to the on-watching crowd. It was believed that attending this spectacle would help people trying to conceive.' Can you imagine?!

3 Monday MAY BANK HOLIDAY

4 Tuesday

'You just can't beat the person who never gives up.' *Babe Ruth*

5 Wednesday

The birthday of Tyrone Power, Michael Palin and Adele!

6 Thursday

7 Friday

8 Saturday

9 Sunday

Spring Veg Focus: Broccoli

Hate broccoli? You're not alone. George Bush Sr once said: 'I haven't liked it since I was a little kid and my mother made me eat it. I'm President of the United States and I'm NOT going to eat any more broccoli.'

Unlike President Bush, I'm a fan of this vegetable and have discovered that it's lovely drizzled in olive oil, salt and pepper and roasted for 20 minutes in a hot oven (425°F/220°C/gas mark 7). It's a revelation, I promise you. If you're not convinced, try boiling it in plenty of salted water for two minutes, then refresh it immediately in ice-cold water. That takes away the tree-like texture and keeps it lovely and green – perfect in salads. Otherwise, steaming keeps it fresh. Pop a few cm of water into the bottom of your steamer, bring it to a simmer – *before* adding the broccoli – pop the broccoli into the basket and steam for 4–5 minutes. I also love it in pasta. I cook it for about five minutes (if it's softer, it absorbs the sauce better), then add half a teaspoon of chilli flakes, cooked pasta, a couple of crushed anchovies and a squeeze of lemon juice. A slug of the cooking water and a sprinkling of parmesan and your delicious pasta dinner is ready.

10 Monday

11 Tuesday

12 Wednesday

Make the most of the longer evenings by getting out and about after dinner. Just 20 minutes outdoors is enough to replenish our reserves of vitamin D.

13 Thursday

14 Friday

15 Saturday

16 Sunday

17 Monday

'When your children are teenagers, it's important to have a dog, so that someone in the house is happy to see you.' *Nora Ephron*

18 Tuesday

Time to refresh your wardrobe. Every year, I take everything out, sort it, try it on and decide what's staying and what's going. Tip: if you haven't worn it for a year, out it goes.

19 Wednesday

20 Thursday

21 Friday

22 Saturday

23 Sunday

Keeping It Green

If you're going to do a big spring clear-out, how do you keep it green? A few pointers:

- *Buy less.* I used to be a collector of all kinds of 'stuff', until I came to sell my house last year and had to do a big clear-out. Never in my life have I come across such a mountain of things that I didn't need and couldn't even remember buying.
- *Recycle as you go.* Any tax documents older than five years and other documents like old bank statements, bills and receipts can be recycled. You can hire a mobile shredder: a man turns up in a flatbed truck which houses a shredder, you hand him your bags and he shreds in front of you. A brilliant idea if you have confidential documents.
- *Cosmetics.* Some brands allow you to return their packaging to the store. Consult www.terracycle.com/en-IE/brigades so you can see who takes what and where. And many of them offer lovely rewards, so it pays to recycle.
- *Plastic bottles.* Don't rinse them, wipe them. I used to religiously rinse my bottles, until I learned that I was releasing all kinds of things into the water. Now I give them a good wipe before putting in the recycling.

24 Monday

'In any moment of decision, the best thing you can do is the right thing. The next best thing is the wrong thing. The worst thing you can do is nothing.' *Theodore Roosevelt*

25 Tuesday

26 Wednesday

When I'm at home, I like to do my housekeeping – paying bills and ringing up about insurance and that sort of thing – once a week. I just give it half an hour, so I don't go mad hanging on the phone listening to music for ever, then I get on with my day. Job done!

27 Thursday

28 Friday

29 Saturday

30 Sunday

Asparagus is my favourite at this time of year. Griddled on a hot pan until it's nice and charred, drizzled with olive oil and with a few shavings of parmesan, it's a treat.

Joyous June

June is my favourite time of year, when the bright evenings seem to go on for ever. I try to make the most of them, because after Midsummer's Day, it's all downhill! At this time of year I'm out in the garden as much as I can be, and the jobs seem endless, between mowing the lawn, weeding, deadheading and watering. If you don't have a big garden, as many of us don't, there are still plenty of things you can do in a yard or balcony. But check first that your balcony can bear the weight of heavy pots!

I love those vertical plant pockets that you hang on a wall. They are great for little ferns and herbs and you can train tomatoes, peas and peppers to grow up a bamboo cane or trellis. But don't try too much. Attempt one or two things at a time to see what grows best in your space. I once saw a vertical garden made out of rows of guttering, which was such a good idea. They had plenty of holes for drainage, which is key in vertical gardens.

31 Monday

'Strive not to be a success, but rather to be of value.' *Albert Einstein*

June

1 Tuesday

---

2 Wednesday

---

3 Thursday

---

4 Friday

---

5 Saturday

Have you ever tried strawberries in a salad? I promise you, they're a revelation. Sliced thinly onto green leaves with little chunks of goat's cheese in a balsamic dressing, they are delicious.

---

6 Sunday

The Retro Housewife

My mother, like so many women of her era, spent a lot of time doing housework. Washing clothes was a huge deal at the time, without a washing machine, and I can remember her peering out of the window anxiously on Mondays to see if there would be 'good drying' after the wash was complete. Dinner was served in the middle of the day and we all came home for it – my brother Damien and myself would traipse home from the Christian Brothers in Westland Row to Dundrum for lunch, which involved two buses, then we'd race back to school for afternoon classes. I can remember Mum leaving hot desserts to cool down on the back step so we could gobble them up before running for the bus to town!

When I was researching this diary, I came across a sample schedule that a 1950s housewife would have kept. It contained no fewer than 38 items! Included was greeting her husband 'gayly' when he returned from work, exercising and applying makeup not once but twice daily, as well as tidying every room in the house, making three meals, which often included dessert, doing the shopping and getting ready her husband's newspaper, drink and cigarettes in readiness for his return. I can't imagine any modern woman having the time to do all that!

7 Monday JUNE BANK HOLIDAY

8 Tuesday

'Ar scáth a chéile a mhaireann na daoine.' ('Under the shelter of each other, people survive.')

9 Wednesday

10 Thursday

11 Friday

Vinegar is a wonder around the house, but beware! Certain surfaces such as stone, marble, hardwood and mahogany do not like this acid. Use the most gentle cleaners you have on these materials.

12 Saturday

13 Sunday

14 Monday

'Start where you are. Use what you have. Do what you can.'
Arthur Ashe

15 Tuesday

16 Wednesday

Many students will be halfway through their exams. Take it easy on them; they have enough stress. Tell them they are doing brilliantly and that the end is in sight.

17 Thursday

18 Friday

19 Saturday

20 Sunday

FRANCIS'S FASCINATING FACTS

Midsummer

This is absolutely my favourite time of year. In Kerry it hardly gets dark at all, even though it marks the end of the long evenings, which always makes me a bit sad. I don't think we realise how lucky we are in the northern hemisphere to have so much summer daylight.

Our pagan ancestors lit bonfires to keep evil at bay, a tradition which we now know as St John's Eve. This year, it's on 23 June. We still light bonfires in Kerry and you can see lots of little puffs of smoke rising into the summer air. Interestingly, many countries have beliefs about the healing powers of herbs, and according to one of my favourite books, *Old Moore's Almanac*, in ancient Ireland, Bulgaria and Denmark, they were considered to be more potent if they were picked on the morning of the solstice. In Estonia, you had to jump over the bonfire for good luck. In Italy, firework displays are held in many cities to celebrate the feast of St John the Baptist. Flower wreaths or crowns are very popular in many European countries and in Norway you can even arrange a mock wedding! Sweden is probably the heart of midsummer traditions, and they decorate a maypole with greenery and flowers and dance around it, singing a song about frogs! It's called 'Små Grodorna', apparently ...

21 Monday

'You should never be ashamed to admit you have been wrong. It only proves you are wiser today than yesterday.' *Jonathan Swift*

22 Tuesday

23 Wednesday

24 Thursday MIDSUMMER'S DAY

Many of us baked bread last year, with varying degrees of success. I found that if I kept a careful eye on the yeast, it all worked out fine. When you add your yeast to lukewarm water with a teaspoon of sugar, give it a stir and leave it for a moment. If it froths, it's fine. If it's flat, ditch it and start again.

25 Friday

26 Saturday

27 Sunday

Salad Days

I love a salad in June, but it has to be easy to put together. There's nothing wrong with the salads we used to eat as children, with the slices of ham, hard-boiled egg, tomato and spring onions – but nowadays we have so many delicious ingredients it seems a shame not to use them.

- I love grilled halloumi with chunks of melon or roasted butternut squash.
- Don't be afraid to use fruit in salads, or nuts (if there are no allergies in the house). Grilled peaches with rocket and Parma ham is delicious.
- In this country, we love coleslaw, but for a change, try fennel and grapefruit, or purple cabbage instead of green, or a vinaigrette dressing instead of mayo. Pumpkin and sunflower seeds are also delicious, as is a handful of chopped coriander for that peppery taste.
- Poached cold salmon is delicious on a bed of couscous, mixed grains or those lovely green lentils – and it's super healthy!

28 Monday

'Success is not final, failure is not fatal: it is the courage to continue that counts.' *Anonymous*

29 Tuesday

30 Wednesday

My moonlight-swimming friend tells me that it has all kinds of benefits. Ireland has so many fantastic places to swim, but remember, the water is *cold*. Don't go alone, stay within your depth, check carefully for any currents and swim parallel to the shore. Enjoy!

July

1 Thursday

2 Friday

3 Saturday

4 Sunday INDEPENDENCE DAY, USA

The art of self-care might
seem very 21st century,
but with our busy lives,
making just half an hour for
ourselves is so important.
We can rest, recharge and
spend time doing things we
love, whether that's walking
the dog, making a cake or
reading or listening to a
good book.

Holiday Planning

Holidays are precious. I'm lucky enough that our hotel winter holiday happens in January. We all head off for a week somewhere nice, all the staff at the Park Hotel Kenmare, which always gives me something to look forward to. We have such a good laugh together and I always come back refreshed and ready for action. I understand that not everyone is as lucky, but if it's any consolation, the summer season is so busy that neither John nor myself has a moment to even think of a break. For you lucky souls who take a summer holiday, whether it's camping in Wexford or a week in Tenerife, here are a few tips:

- Set your budget first. Don't get annoyed because the States is out of the question: focus on what you *can* do. Try not to pick a holiday in Mexico and then stress about how you're going to pay for it. See how doing this in reverse works out.
- When I was a child, holidays were spent at Granny's in County Sligo, helping on her little farm. Coming from suburban Dublin, it was a treat to feed hens and to churn real butter. Sometimes the simplest experiences are the best.
- If you're planning a 'staycation', prepare as if you're actually going away. Plan how long you're going 'away' for, tell everyone that you are not at work (so no emails!) and book in an activity every day, whether it's a cycle ride, visiting a museum, taking a train ride, a hike up the mountains ... behave as if you are on your holidays and you'll soon feel that you are!

5 Monday

'You are never too old to set another goal or to dream a new dream.' *C.S. Lewis*

6 Tuesday

7 Wednesday

When I was in India on the Grand Tour, I lost a lot of weight. When I came home, it was a challenge to keep it off, so I just focused on making small changes to my diet. Porridge for breakfast, brown bread instead of white and no eating late at night. I stuck to these rules and managed to mostly stay on the wagon!

8 Thursday

9 Friday

10 Saturday

11 Sunday

Saving Water

I used to use water as if there was an everlasting spring of the stuff, but now I'm much more careful. I save 'grey' water for my plants, I don't run the tap until I've finished brushing my teeth and so on. We all think that we have plenty of water in this country, and lord knows it rains, but even so we have to try harder for the environment's sake.

- I have a friend who has a busy household with four teenagers in it. Can you imagine the showers? She installed a little timer in the shower and set it to four minutes, after which it would beep loudly. You might laugh, but a shower uses ten litres of water a *minute*, so that's some saving.
- www.water.ie suggests that we don't run the tap for a cold drink, but fill a jug and keep it in the fridge instead. Why didn't I think of that? It also reminded me that flushing the loo uses a huge amount of water. 'If it's yellow, let it mellow,' they say!
- I try not to use a hose in the garden any more, because I know that it wastes water. I have a barrel at the side of the house to collect rainwater and I save any rinsing water for the plants, as well as using a watering can. I really try to avoid lawn sprinklers.

12 Monday

'Before you marry someone, you should first make them use a computer with slow internet to see who they really are.' *Will Ferrell*

13 Tuesday

14 Wednesday

Bastille Day in France, or *le 14 juillet*, commemorates the storming of the Bastille by the revolutionaries against Louis XVI. It is also celebrated in New Orleans.

15 Thursday

16 Friday

17 Saturday

18 Sunday

19 Monday

'Almost everything will work again if you unplug it for a few minutes. Including you.' *Anne Lamott*

20 Tuesday

21 Wednesday

22 Thursday

A summer fruit crumble is a delicious way to use up unripe or overripe fruit. I like to use a mix of berries, peaches, apricots and other summer fruits, to which I add a good squeeze of orange juice, an ounce or two of sugar (50g) and a dusting of cinnamon or mixed spice. Pop on a crumble topping and into the oven for 20 minutes at 190°C/ 375°F/gas mark 5.

23 Friday

24 Saturday

25 Sunday

Enjoy Yourself

Because I was at home for a long time last year – the longest I've ever been home for many years – I had to learn to enjoy myself more, in spite of everything else that was going on. At first, I thought that I'd use all that free time to sort my jumpers, clear my closets and organise my tableware, but when I opened a drawer and discovered ten different sets of napkins, I decided it was time to stop!

Instead, I began to think about what I really enjoyed in life now that I couldn't travel, or zip up to Dublin for a meeting, or even run around the hotel annoying everyone! First of all, I realised that just sitting in the garden on a sunny day could be nice; next, I stopped giving out to myself if I felt bored or upset – it's not natural to be dancing with happiness all of the time – so if I got fed up, I'd just deal with it. Finally, instead of fussing about what might happen in six months' time, I just asked myself, 'What do I want to do today?' And if the answer was 'nothing much', well, I sat down on the sofa with a cup of tea and a book. It really is the simple things in life that make it worthwhile.

26 Monday

'One must maintain a little bit of
summer even in the middle of winter.'
Henry David Thoreau

27 Tuesday

28 Wednesday

29 Thursday

I've been trying to be kinder to wildlife
in my garden. I leave the hedge alone, so
as not to disturb birds, and I have sown
bee-friendly plants, such as lavender. A
friend of mine also leaves out a little dish of
cat food (in a safe place) for hedgehogs!

30 Friday

31 Saturday

August

1 Sunday

An August Midnight

A shaded lamp and a waving blind,
And the beat of a clock from a distant floor;
On this scene enter – winged, horned, and spined –
A longlegs, a moth, and a dumbledore*;
While 'mid my page there idly stands
A sleepy fly that rubs its hands ...

Thus meet we five, in this still place
At this point of time, at this point in space.
– My guests besmear my new-penned line,
Or bang at the lamp and fall supine.
'God's humblest, they!' I muse. Yet why?
They know Earth-secrets that know not I.

Thomas Hardy

* bumblebee

2 Monday AUGUST BANK HOLIDAY

3 Tuesday

4 Wednesday

'Dá fhada an lá, tagann an tráthnóna.' ('No matter how long the day, the evening comes.')

5 Thursday

At this stage, my garden is looking a little tired, so I do a little bit of tidying, cutting back old foliage and yellowing leaves, even if it reminds me that autumn is almost here. To cheer myself up, I plant some seeds for winter veg: cabbage, kale, beetroot, carrots, chard, so I have something to put in the pot when the days are darker.

6 Friday

7 Saturday

8 Sunday

A Late Summer Picnic

When I was a child we used to love picnics, when Mum would pack a wicker hamper with ham sandwiches, hard-boiled eggs, fruit cake and a big flask of sweetened tea. Food tasted even more delicious because we were eating outside, even if it was blowing a gale! Nowadays, picnics can be very sophisticated affairs, but I think simple is often best, because it leaves you with more time to enjoy yourself.

There's nothing I like better than a sausage roll, but for all of you vegans out there, finely chopped mushrooms, sautéed until the flavour really develops, a drop or two of soy sauce or miso paste, if you have it, a pinch of dried herbs, salt and pepper and a handful of breadcrumbs makes for a lovely filling. If you don't want to make vegan pastry, there are supermarket versions available – just look for the non-butter variety.

A lovely recipe I discovered recently is muhammara. This roast red pepper dip can be made with roasted red peppers from a jar or a couple of red peppers that you've roasted. Add 50g chopped walnuts, a clove or two of garlic, a teaspoon of cumin and a pinch of red chilli flakes. The recipe also calls for 1tbsp pomegranate molasses, which is concentrated pomegranate juice. If you can't find any, cranberry juice concentrate will work. Pop everything into your food processor, add enough olive oil to loosen the mixture and blitz. It's delicious.

9 Monday

'In three words, I can sum up
everything I've learned about life:
it goes on.' *Robert Frost*

10 Tuesday

11 Wednesday

12 Thursday

13 Friday

I'm not superstitious, but I always
pause a little on this date! If I lived
in Spain, however, I'd be worried
on Tuesday the 13th and in Italy, on
Friday the 17th. And the word for fear
of this day is friggatriskaidekaphobia!

14 Saturday

15 Sunday

16 Monday

'A person who never
made a mistake never
tried anything new.'
Albert Einstein

17 Tuesday

18 Wednesday

19 Thursday

The birthday of Coco
Chanel, Bill Clinton and
inventor Orville Wright

20 Friday

21 Saturday

22 Sunday

The New School Year

When I was a child, we'd begin to get anxious at this time of year, because we'd be back at school in a fortnight. The long summer evenings would be over and it would be time to get back to the books. I can still remember my mother taking us to Fred Hanna's in Dublin to get our schoolbooks. The shop stocked quite a lot of second-hand books, but I'd be praying for new, because they looked so much nicer, the pages bright and crisp. We used to cover them with brown paper, I recall. A friend of mine says that her mother made her cover hers with wallpaper, big thick vinyl with a floral pattern on it, which was certainly hard-wearing!

I wasn't a particularly academic child, so even though I didn't misbehave, I daydreamed a lot and my reports left something to be desired. In the course of my research, I came across some amusing report cards. Richard Branson was told that he 'would either go to prison or become a millionaire'. Albert Einstein was told 'he would never amount to anything', and my favourite, about Stephen Fry: 'Stephen has glaring faults and they have certainly glared at us this term.'

23 Monday

'With the new day comes new strength and new thoughts.'
Eleanor Roosevelt

24 Tuesday

25 Wednesday

26 Thursday

27 Friday

Herbs are some of my favourite plants to grow. All they need is sun, shelter from the wind, good drainage and regular light watering.

28 Saturday

29 Sunday

I've always found mindfulness difficult to embrace. I'm a great man for taking each day as it comes, but I find it very hard to slow down. A few things work for me, though: audiobooks are great, particularly those read by the author – it's like having a bedtime story for adults! Find whatever works for you and bring it in to your life daily.

Getting It Together

I've always had my own system when it comes to organising. I have a large manila envelope and when I think of something, I write it down on a piece of paper, which I put into the envelope. I have a small diary into which I write an entry every day, even if it's just a line or two. I put meetings into my phone calendar and, of course, mark out any holidays. And that's it! It might not sound like the most sophisticated system, but it works for me.

I had the sad task, along with my brothers and sisters, of clearing out Mum's home in Sligo when she died last year. The one thing I learned was to put emotions to one side when I was looking at all the tablecloths and sets of napkins Mum had, or her favourite winter coat. I hadn't looked at them in a long time, but things can have such emotions attached to them, I find. I knew that if filled a wardrobe with her clothing, I would simply be putting off the difficult task of saying goodbye to her, so, with a heavy heart, I decided to just take one or two small mementos. I came across a little notebook, covered in brown paper, in which she'd written 'notaí gaeilge', in her immaculate handwriting, a series of poems and little sayings in Irish. Now, every time I take the notebook out, I think of her, and that means more to me than a pile of jumpers or sets of cutlery. It is just enough.

30 Monday

'Take the first step in faith. You don't have to see the whole staircase, just take the first step.' *Martin Luther King Jr*

31 Tuesday

September

1 Wednesday

2 Thursday

I used to both dread and look forward to a new year in school. It was a chance to turn the page and start afresh. I still have that feeling in early September every year, so I look on it as an opportunity to start a new project.

3 Friday

4 Saturday

5 Sunday

Vinegar ~ A Cleaning Wonder

While browsing my stock of books for this diary, I came across a note about the many uses of vinegar in home cleaning – by vinegar I mean the white, distilled variety.

- *In laundry* – add 275ml/10fl.oz vinegar to your washing machine to give your clothes an extra clean: and it's great for keeping lint at bay, too. Also, if your whites are turning yellow, instead of using harmful bleach, try soaking them in warm water and vinegar (1 part vinegar to 12 parts water) overnight. Pop them in the washing machine and no more yucky yellow.
- *In home cleaning* – 1 part vinegar to 2 parts water in a spray bottle makes a great quick cleaner. Use it as a surface cleaner. There's no getting away from the smell – but I open the windows afterwards to let the air in.
- *In pet care* – a mix of 1 part vinegar to 2 parts water makes a great pet-cage cleaner; it's also brilliant for cleaning cat litter trays, I'm told. And if you have a dog, use half a cup of vinegar in your machine's rinse cycle when washing blankets and cushions – it's brilliant for getting rid of that doggy smell!

6 Monday

'Is olc an ghaoth nach séideann maith do dhuine éigin.'
('It's a bad wind that doesn't blow good for someone.')

7 Tuesday

8 Wednesday

9 Thursday

10 Friday

11 Saturday

Are you a poor sleeper? I used to be a great man for sending texts and messages at one o'clock in the morning after a day at the hotel. I called it 'catching up' until I realised that it was keeping me awake. Now I leave my phone in the living room and wake myself up with a good old-fashioned alarm clock.

12 Sunday

13 Monday

'There are some things one can only achieve by a deliberate leap in the opposite direction.'
Franz Kafka

---

14 Tuesday

---

15 Wednesday

---

16 Thursday

I change my summer duvet for my winter one at around this time. I pull the winter duvet out of the wardrobe and discover that I didn't wash it before I put it away. Try to remember to wash your duvets and, even more important, air them before changing them. Do as I say, not as I do!

---

17 Friday

---

18 Saturday

---

19 Sunday

Apples and Blackberries

One of my favourite things to do as a child was picking blackberries, staining everything purple in the process! We also had to pick apples from one of our neighbours' gardens, and I can still smell the apples, which we stored carefully in a huge plastic barrel, separated by sheets of newspaper. Now I look forward to the days when the hedgerows will be filled with the fruit and cars will stop by the side of the road for people to pick a few. Here are a few ideas for this delicious combination.

I love a compote, made of 250g/10oz cooking apples and 175g/6oz blackberries, depending on what proportions you like. I add a couple of tablespoons of sugar and a little water, just to stop it from burning, and cook until softened – about 10 minutes. It's lovely – even with a pork chop. I also love to adapt my favourite pineapple upside-down cake with blackberries and chopped cooking apples. I place half of the chopped, washed fruit (about 450g or 16oz in total) at the bottom of my greased 20cm/8 inch cake tin, sprinkle over the sugar, then make a sponge topping with 125g unsalted butter, 125g caster sugar and 125g self-raising flour. I cream the butter and sugar together until fluffy, then add a drop or two of vanilla essence, before adding the flour and folding it in – I loosen with a tablespoon of milk if it's a bit stiff. I gently add the remaining fruit, then put the mixture into the tin, even it up and pop into an oven at 160°C/325°F/ gas mark 4. Forty minutes later – it's ready.

20 Monday

'Every man is sociable until a cow invades his garden.' This old Irish saying means that we all have days when nothing goes according to plan.

21 Tuesday

22 Wednesday

23 Thursday

24 Friday

25 Saturday

26 Sunday

Home Composting

Talking about compost always reminds me of our handyman, Cyril, who used to help out around my childhood home in Balally. At the time, many households would have had a constant stream of 'little men' who turned up to clean the windows and do other odd jobs around the place. Cyril was from County Offaly, as I recall, and he used to go home every now and then, cycling all the way on his bike. Can you imagine? Anyway, he used to do a couple of jobs for the local nuns and in exchange, he'd be given two big buckets of manure, which he'd carry up through the town – the smell must have been something else – before emptying them onto his roses. Whenever he got a compliment about them, he'd say, 'Ah, sure you can't beat the nuns' sh*te'!

On the subject of 'sh*te', I've become a great man for compositing, ever since a nephew gave me a wormery. It takes a little bit of time to get used to, but it's brilliant for household veg peelings, old tea bags, egg cartons and even strips of newspaper. You get a little supply of worms to start off – and instructions – and before you know it, you have a steaming pile of you-know-what of your own, as the worms chomp through all that organic waste. Don't put meat into it, though – you'll get more than worms if you do! There are home-composting systems that take animal waste, but the wormery is best used for vegetable and fruit peelings.

27 Monday

'I've a great fancy to see my own funeral afore I die.' *Maria Edgeworth*, Castle Rackrent

28 Tuesday

29 Wednesday

30 Thursday

Once September comes to an end, I start thinking about bulbs. There's nothing I like better than seeing a variety of tulips, daffodils and crocuses springing to life in a few months' time. — *October*

1 Friday

2 Saturday

3 Sunday

*I used to be an awful man
for saying yes to everything,
but now I have learned that
it's okay to say no every now
and then. If you find it hard,
say 'I'll think about that'
to buy some time to reflect.
Then say no with less guilt!*

Bit of a Pickle

When I was a child, I had an uncle who used to love pickled onions. He would eat them by the jarful, and I've always associated that vinegary smell with him. Nowadays, pickling is all the rage again, thanks partly to Asian cooking, such as Korean cuisine, which uses a lot of pickling and fermenting, and a desire to be more sustainable.

You can pickle more or less anything, but veg such as green beans, peppers and cauliflower are great, as are cucumbers and red cabbage – and they look wonderful. I find that pickling a red onion really softens the taste of it, too. A basic pickle involves simmering equal quantities of water and vinegar (white wine, cider, apple, plain – avoid balsamic as it'll drown the veg), adding a tablespoon of salt and a tablespoon of sugar – then your herbs and spices of choice. Ginger is good, as is a bay leaf, peppercorns, even garlic if you like it.

My stalwart *Country Wisdom & Know-How* tells me that commercial vinegar is best for preserving, because home-made vinegars might not be strong enough to preserve properly. Be careful pouring the pickling liquid into whatever jar you are going to use – it will be hot. I always put the jar in the sink to fill it up, just in case. Also, make sure there are no air bubbles in the jar by poking around with a skewer or chopstick. This will make the lid seal more tightly. Watch out for any bubbles that might appear, or anything that might indicate the presence of bacteria. Make sure that you use modern, tested recipes to ensure that food safety is a priority.

4 Monday

'The world is full of magic things, patiently waiting for our senses to grow sharper.' *W.B. Yeats*

5 Tuesday

6 Wednesday

I love making a big pot of butternut squash or pumpkin soup. I chop the veg, then roast it for 30 minutes in a hot oven for better flavour, and add a pinch of chilli flakes or ground coriander to my softened onions for a little kick. A litre of stock, a nice simmer for 20 minutes, then blitz.

7 Thursday

8 Friday

9 Saturday

10 Sunday

11 Monday

'Start by doing what is necessary; then do what's possible: and suddenly you are doing the impossible.'
St Francis of Assisi

12 Tuesday

13 Wednesday

14 Thursday

Now is a good time to take up a new hobby to keep you going during the long winter months. A friend of mine has taught himself fly-tying, another has taken up hillwalking and another is learning Spanish. These might not float your boat, but what about something else? Make sure it's fun, so you'll stick with it.

15 Friday

16 Saturday

17 Sunday

Preparing for Winter

At the Park Hotel Kenmare, October marks the end of our busy season, so we begin planning any improvements or refurbishments to be carried out during the winter months. In a hotel there is always something to be done to keep up with the market. We also begin some Christmas preparations. Shane, the gardener, will have been collecting pinecones, which we put in the boiler room to dry for our Christmas wreath, along with slices of orange, which we've dried at a low temperature in the oven. We also use them in the wreath, along with the cones, some cloves, a twist of cinnamon sticks, as well as ferns and holly from the garden. Shane also has a good stock of tree branches with lovely lichen on them, which we dry out and keep to decorate the door lintels. All very sustainable. Keep an eye out for any attractive natural flora that you can use in your own winter display.

18 Monday

19 Tuesday

20 Wednesday

Mushrooms are plentiful at this time of year, and I remember setting out on damp mornings, a bucket in my hand, to collect them. We confined ourselves to field mushrooms, I suspect because we knew they were safe to eat. I envy our Eastern European neighbours who know everything about foraging! Mushrooms always remind me of autumn.

21 Thursday

22 Friday

23 Saturday

24 Sunday

Hallowe'en

There are variations of this festival all over the world, but what they all have in common is a ritual of remembering the dead. In ancient Ireland, Samhain marked the dividing line between the light of summer and the darkness of winter. It was rumoured that, because the dividing line between this world and the other world was thin at this time of year, spirits could pass through. People dressed up in masks and costumes to disguise themselves from any bad spirits that might want to hang around! Today, we have the Hallowe'en Howl in Kenmare, a week-long festival that really draws in the crowds.

Bonfires were another feature of the festival and people would leave out food for the dead, including sometimes bowls of mashed potato and cabbage, which is believed to be the origins of colcannon. Many festivals in other parts of the world involve remembering our ancestors, such as Día de los Muertos in Mexico, and the festival of the Hungry Ghost in China, where food is also left out. In this country we would have been familiar with the *púca*, the ghostly figure who was rumoured to appear at Hallowe'en – indeed, the tradition is being revived as a festival by Fáilte Ireland – but the *dullahan* was another matter – a headless man on a horse, carrying his head in his hands. If you saw him on Hallowe'en, it was curtains for you!

25 Monday

'I don't think of all the misery, but of the beauty that still remains.' *Anne Frank*

26 Tuesday

27 Wednesday

28 Thursday

When I was a child, the barmbrack my mother made would contain more than just a ring. She'd put in a sixpence (to signify wealth), a piece of twig (you'd have a row with someone), a little scrap of material (you'd be poor) and even a pea (you wouldn't marry). We used to have a great time trying to predict where the ring was in the cake.

29 Friday

30 Saturday

31 Sunday HALLOWE'EN

Finding time to just 'be'
at this time of year can
be hard. Set an alarm
on your phone for, say,
mid-afternoon, and when
it goes off, give yourself
five minutes to catch up
with yourself. How are you
feeling today? If 'not great'
is the answer, ask yourself
why and what small thing
you could do to make
yourself feel better.

Feeding the Birds

Looking after feathered visitors to the garden really cheers me up in November, when it can be so cold and grey. I spend a fortune on bird food and I've collected all sorts of feeders over the years. I prefer to focus on the smaller birds and leave the magpies and crows to look after themselves.

- Peanuts are a great source of calories for birds, but don't use those mesh bags that they sometimes come in as they can get their little feet caught in them. Empty the peanuts into a wire peanut feeder.
- Mixed seeds are fine, but I'm told that the cheaper varieties will attract sparrows, which might explain why I have a big gang of them, and not other kinds of birds. Robins, in particular, love mealworms. I got a big container of dried mealworms from my DIY store and put them on a little shelf that the robins love.
- A suet block is a sure-fire winner, but don't leave it out on your bird table – every time I have, I discovered something furry shinning up the bird table to steal it! Now I have one of those suet-block holders, which works a treat.

1 Monday ALL SAINTS' DAY

'Love all, trust a few, do wrong to none.'
William Shakespeare, All's Well That Ends Well

2 Tuesday ALL SOULS' DAY

3 Wednesday

4 Thursday

5 Friday

6 Saturday

7 Sunday

Annette's Christmas Cake

At the Park Hotel Kenmare, we make a rich fruitcake for our guests who spend every Christmas with us, and every day or two James, the head chef, pours brandy into the little holes. By the time it gets to the big day, it's very boozy. Here's a nice recipe from a friend's mother-in-law – thank you, Annette!

Ingredients

225g/8oz sultanas
225g/8oz raisins
225g/8oz currants
115g/4oz chopped figs
50g/2oz halved glacé cherries
50g/2oz crystallised ginger
45ml/2tbsp brandy (or whiskey)
225g plain flour
pinch salt

½tsp cinnamon
½tsp grated nutmeg
1tsp cocoa powder
225g/8oz butter
225g/8oz dark brown sugar
4 large eggs
grated rind of 1 lemon/orange
50g/2oz ground almonds
50g/2oz chopped walnuts

Method

1. The night before you bake, soak the dried fruit in the brandy/whiskey. Leave to plump overnight.
2. Grease and line a 20cm/8in cake tin. Preheat the oven to 160°C/325°F/gas mark 3.
3. Sift together the dry ingredients.
4. Whisk the butter and sugar together until light and fluffy. Gradually beat in the eggs. Mix in the lemon/orange zest, ground almonds, chopped walnuts and dried fruit, then finally the dry ingredients.
5. Pour the mixture into the tin and gently tap in on the kitchen counter to get rid of any bubbles. Place in the oven for 3 hours, or until a skewer inserted into it comes out clean. Allow the cake to cool in the tin for an hour, then gently remove and place it on a wire rack.

8 Monday

9 Tuesday

10 Wednesday

At this time of year at the hotel, we pop our pots of hyacinth bulbs into the hot press to force them, so they'll be ready for the guests' bedrooms at Christmas time. Amaryllis is another favourite.

11 Thursday

12 Friday

13 Saturday

14 Sunday

15 Monday

'The personal life deeply lived always expands into truths beyond itself.' *Anaïs Nin*

16 Tuesday

17 Wednesday

18 Thursday

19 Friday

20 Saturday

21 Sunday

Stir-up Sunday. 'Stir up, we beseech thee, O Lord, the wills of thy faithful people.' This prayer was usually said on the Sunday before Advent, hence the name. Mum used to make the Christmas pudding around now. She'd give each of us a turn at stirring it and making a wish and I can still remember the smell of whiskey and spices that would fill the kitchen.

A Pre-Christmas Tidy

Whether or not you're a lover of the season, it can be really worthwhile to give the house a good clean at this time of year. With the windows closed, it can get stuffy and dusty, and the radiators make the air dry. Also, if your dog or cat friends are indoors more, there can be a lovely build-up of hair around the place – and what guest likes that at Christmas?

- I use the pointed attachment on my hoover to reach up into cobwebby corners, or you can tie a microfibre cloth to a dry mop with an elastic band to make an extra-long duster. You can also use this around door and window frames.
- Take Fido outside to brush him and, while you're at it, clean his bedding.
- Work your way down, not up, so you don't end up with dust falling all over your newly polished shelving.
- If something is very dusty, I run over the surface with a dry cloth, then use a damp one to get rid of stickiness, before drying it with a paper towel. Don't use a damp cloth on wood, though – you'll end up with water stains.

22 Monday

23 Tuesday

24 Wednesday

25 Thursday

26 Friday

27 Saturday

28 Sunday

Planning Ahead for a Budget-friendly Christmas

We all go overboard at Christmas, but for some of us it can be a source of real worry and stress. No wonder we all get so down in January when the credit-card bill comes in. Here are a few tips to reduce your spending:

- *Buy in advance.* This year, every time I stopped outside a shop and said, 'Oh, so-and-so would like that,' I have then gone into the shop and bought it. I now have a nice pile at the bottom of my wardrobe, so I won't have a mad dash around at Christmas.
- Do you buy a new set of fairy lights every season and go home to find you already have four? Time to *make an inventory* of everything you already have, before purchasing more.
- *Don't buy gifts for the world and his wife.* Make a list of the people you really want to give a present to – or, better still, do Kris Kindle, as we do in my family. One adult, two children – and that's it!
- *Re-purpose last year's Christmas outfit* – you'll probably only have worn it a couple of times and it's more sustainable. As a man with a million suits, I've really been trying hard to follow my own advice!

29 Monday

'Breathe. Let go. And remind yourself that this very moment is the only one you know you have for sure.'
Oprah Winfrey

30 Tuesday

December

1 Wednesday

2 Thursday

3 Friday

4 Saturday

5 Sunday

Christmas Drinks for Everyone

I love the smell of mulled wine, even though I'm not a drinker. There's something about that warm, spicy smell that says Christmas to me. Nowadays, you can buy sachets of spices, a bit like a teabag, to pop into your warm red wine, or you can simply add a couple of sticks of cinnamon, a few cloves, some orange slices and a couple of star anise, along with some honey. Warm the wine gently and, if you like, add a shot of brandy when you take it off the heat. Espresso martinis are another new favourite and they look wonderful. At the hotel we use 25ml/1fl. oz of fresh espresso coffee, twice as much vodka, 25ml/1fl. oz of coffee liqueur and 15ml/3tsp sugar syrup, poured over ice and shaken vigorously. Delicious. If you're a non-drinker, like me, you can have your very own mocktail: elderflower cordial and soda water makes a lovely fake champagne; or go mad on a rich, creamy hot chocolate made with a bar of dark chocolate and cream.

6 Monday

'My idea of Christmas, whether old-fashioned or modern, is very simple: loving others.' *Bob Hope*

7 Tuesday

8 Wednesday

9 Thursday

I like to rummage around in my kitchen drawers around now to see that I have all the things I need for Christmas dinner: mince-pie cutters, seasonal napkins, turkey-roasting tray, candles, table decorations and so on. I'm always surprised at how much I have, but it also gives me time to buy anything that's missing.

10 Friday

11 Saturday

12 Sunday

13 Monday

'As you grow older, you
will discover that you have
two hands, one for helping
yourself, the other for
helping others.' *Sam Levenson*

14 Tuesday

15 Wednesday

Instead of multi-tasking, try
single-tasking – doing one
thing at a time! If I try to do
more than a couple of things
in a day, I go half-mad – and
I forget what's important.

16 Thursday

17 Friday

18 Saturday

19 Sunday

Christmas With the Family

Christmas can be a bit of a pressure cooker for families. Adult children reunited at home can end up behaving as they did when they were seven; we get exhausted going up and down the stairs to bring Granny up a cup of tea or a hot-water bottle; and guests settle in for the afternoon, unaware that you'd really like them to leave.

1. Remember, Christmas is just one day in a whole year, so try to be on your best behaviour – remind yourself it's only 24 hours.

2. Focus on the now with your siblings and parents, not on twenty years ago. If your brother starts teasing you about your childhood habits, very politely bring the conversation around to his job, or a great holiday you took recently.

3. Take it in turns to 'do' Christmas if your parents are elderly. It's not fair to ask them to do it every year.

4. Christmas is for children. Don't make them wait all day to open their presents so that they become cranky and tired.

5. Don't overdo the booze on an empty stomach! My friends tell me that it's a killer. Wait until the meal to start, when you'll have a nice full tummy.

20 Monday

'I will honour Christmas in my heart, and try to keep it all the year.' *Charles Dickens*, A Christmas Carol

21 Tuesday

22 Wednesday

23 Thursday

24 Friday CHRISTMAS EVE

25 Saturday CHRISTMAS DAY

26 Sunday ST STEPHEN'S DAY

In Kerry, we have a long tradition of 'Wren's Day', or 'Wran's Day' as it's sometimes called. Traditionally, this celebration would involve dressing up in straw costumes, which people still do in Dingle. There's fierce competition between the different groups to have the best displays – all in the aid of charity.

The New Year

On New Year's Eve we push the boat out at the hotel with a big party. We pin a huge net of balloons to the ceiling in the function room, using fishing line to hold it in place. It's easy to quickly snip and watch the balloons fall. And can we ever find the little knife we use to cut the line? John Moriarty, the barman, is a divil for tidying it away, so now we have three of them.

We used to have a band from Cork, I recall, to do the entertainment for the night. Tommy was the bandleader and he used to do the countdown. One New Year's Eve, instead of counting 'ten, nine, eight' and so on, he had a senior moment and started counting 'one, two, three ...' I could see the look of fear and confusion on his face, wondering if he should just keep on going to a hundred or reverse, and the guests didn't know whether to clap along or to just wait.

27 Monday

'The best is yet to come.' *Frank Sinatra*

28 Tuesday

Mum's birthday. Or, at least, we think it was. Mum couldn't remember whether it was the 28th or the 29th! And with the hotel in full swing at this time, it would be a family joke that we'd forget to send her a card. We used to tease her – 'If you had a proper birthday, we'd send you a proper birthday card.' We never did forget her big day, of course.

29 Wednesday

30 Thursday

31 Friday NEW YEAR'S EVE

January

1 Saturday NEW YEAR'S DAY

2 Sunday

Another year has passed, and it's tempting to make a ton of resolutions, but why not focus on what you'd really love to do this year? Visit a friend in France? Go camping in Donegal? Learn Chinese? Whatever it is, make it positive.

ESSENTIAL CONTACTS

Name	
Address	
Mobile	
Email	

Name	
Address	
Mobile	
Email	

Name	
Address	
Mobile	
Email	

Name	
Address	
Mobile	
Email	

Name	
Address	
Mobile	
Email	

Name	
Address	
Mobile	
Email	

Name	
Address	
Mobile	
Email	

Name	
Address	
Mobile	
Email	

Name	
Address	
Mobile	
Email	

Name	
Address	
Mobile	
Email	

Name	
Address	
Mobile	
Email	

Name	
Address	
Mobile	
Email	

Name	
Address	
Mobile	
Email	

Name	
Address	
Mobile	
Email	

Name	
Address	
Mobile	
Email	

Name	
Address	
Mobile	
Email	

Name	
Address	
Mobile	
Email	

Name	
Address	
Mobile	
Email	

Name	
Address	
Mobile	
Email	

Name	
Address	
Mobile	
Email	

NOTES